Evaluating and Developing Administrative Performance

Peter Seldin

Evaluating and Developing Administrative Performance

A Practical Guide for Academic Leaders

 Jossey-Bass Publishers

San Francisco • London • 1988

EVALUATING AND DEVELOPING ADMINISTRATIVE PERFORMANCE
A Practical Guide for Academic Leaders
by Peter Seldin

Copyright © 1988 by: Jossey-Bass Inc., Publishers
350 Sansome Street
San Francisco, California 94104
&
Jossey-Bass Limited
28 Banner Street
London EC1Y 8QE

Library of Congress Cataloging-in-Publication Data

Seldin, Peter.
  Evaluating and developing administrative performance.

  (The Jossey-Bass higher education series)
  Bibliography: p.
  Includes index.
  1. College administrators—United States—
Rating of. I. Title. II. Series.
LB2342.7.S35   1988   378'.11'0973   88-42799
ISBN 1-55542-119-9

Manufactured in the United States of America

The paper in this book meets the guidelines for
permanence and durability of the Committee on
Production Guidelines for Book Longevity of the
Council on Library Resources.

JACKET DESIGN BY WILLI BAUM

FIRST EDITION

Code 8842

Contents

Preface

An important change is taking place in higher education: academic administrators are being held accountable, as never before, for how well they do their jobs. Current interest in appraising administrative performance grows out of the demand by government, the general public, and every sector of the academic community for more accountability. This demand has been fueled by the growing acceptance and use by colleges and universities of management principles that emphasize performance evaluation of administrators and staff.

Why should an institution undertake the difficult, time-consuming, and costly process of systematically evaluating administrative performance? One compelling reason for doing so is to provide a rational and equitable basis for promotion and retention of administrative personnel. With annual salaries plus benefits for senior academic administrators often exceeding $100,000, such personnel decisions can have significant financial implications.

Another important reason is that performance evaluation helps identify areas of professional and personal development that need fine tuning. As a result, both the individual and the institution can benefit. As academic administration becomes more complex and specialized, administrators will increasingly profit from familiarity with state-of-the-art administrative and management practices.

Previous books on evaluating and developing academic

administrators have largely been collections of philosophical essays, often about specific administrative positions, such as the academic dean or department chair. In *Evaluating and Developing Administrative Performance,* I take a different approach: I offer an institutional-level perspective; I discuss the critical legal considerations that affect evaluation systems; the influence of academic culture on programs for and goals of assessing and developing performance; the practices, strategies, and forms currently used by many institutions around the country; and the multiplying development opportunities available on and off campus; and I provide specific examples and detailed descriptions of numerous professional development activities.

Although this book provides readers with a distillation of the relevant research literature, it also does much more in that it reflects the author's personal experience over nearly two decades as an academic dean, department chair, professor of management, and consultant to more than one hundred institutions of higher education in all parts of the country.

Who Should Read This Book

Evaluating and Developing Administrative Performance is intended to provide college and university administrators with useful, research-based information on how to evaluate and improve their own and others' professional performance. The book presents promising new approaches for assessing and developing administrators' potential, practical recommendations for action, and a battery of field-tested forms designed to sharpen administrative skills. My aim is to generate objective and critical thinking and, where necessary, to act as a stimulus for change.

This book was written for trustees, presidents, academic vice-presidents, provosts, deans, department chairs, and faculty leaders—the essential partners in developing successful administrative evaluation and improvement programs. But the ideas presented in this book should prove of value to administrators at all levels in reviewing their present systems and planning revisions. I have included practical, how-to advice and specific discussion of a range of topics, from the problems of effective performance appraisal to strategies for administrative development. The book will also be helpful to students of higher education, especially those planning careers in academic administration.

Overview of the Contents

In Chapter One I discuss the new breed of academic administrators and the assessment and development of their performance, and I explain how the methods selected for the assessment program relate to the academic culture of the institution.

In Chapter Two I investigate the rationale for assessing administrative performance, the connection between an institution's frame of reference and the appraisal of administrative actions, and the deficiencies and other limitations in appraisal programs.

I describe seven key requirements of appraisal systems in Chapter Three. As well, I detail the performance criteria for such systems, the psychometric errors in evaluating performance and how to avoid them, and the advantages and disadvantages of six different approaches to administrator evaluation.

Chapter Four spells out how to plan and implement a viable evaluation system, what should be evaluated, and who should do the evaluating. Also explored are sources of evidence of quality administrative performance, timing, criteria, and the critical connection between evaluation and development. Field-tested appraisal forms are included in the Appendix to Chapter Four.

In Chapter Five I examine the application of civil rights legislation to administrative evaluation programs, assessment criteria and the law, recent court decisions, alternatives to litigation, due process, and preventive law.

In Chapter Six I discuss the role of experience in the professional development of administrators, some desirable and undesirable administrative behaviors and attributes, alternative strategies for enhancing performance, and the implementation of a development program.

In Chapter Seven I explore the development of administrative skills and the in-house activities and external opportunities for teaching those skills, including mentoring, Outward Bound training, workshops, internships, and development programs at particular institutions.

In Chapter Eight I consider the college or university president as a role model for the evaluation and development process; the criteria, methods, and timing of assessment; models of presidential assessment; and specific approaches to professional development.

The Appendix at the end of the book summarizes the key points in evaluating and developing administrative performance.

Acknowledgments

I am grateful to Pace University for providing support for this book through a scholarly research grant. Special thanks go to George Parks, Joseph Pastore, and Frieda Reitman for their unflagging encouragement and assistance. They have been more helpful than they may realize.

I dedicate this book to my parents, Joseph and Rose Seldin, to whom I owe a lifetime of gratitude. My dad read an earlier draft of this manuscript in the hope of guarding the English language from too obvious discord. His ear for the music of good language improved the text. And to my family—my wife, Pat, and our children, Marc, Amy, and Nancy—who are my greatest fortune. They have enriched my life in ways that words cannot convey.

Croton-on-Hudson, New York   Peter Seldin
August 1988

The Author

Peter Seldin is professor of management at Pace University, Pleasantville, New York. He received his B.A. degree (1963) in psychology from Hobart College, his M.B.A. degree (1966) in management from Long Island University, and his Ph.D. degree (1974) in education from Fordham University. He completed his postdoctoral work in evaluation and development at the University of London in 1976.

Seldin has designed and conducted seminars for faculty and administrators in colleges and universities throughout the United States and in Japan, England, Egypt, Switzerland, Israel, and Africa. He is a frequent speaker at national and international conferences. He has served on the editorial board of the quarterly newspaper *Faculty Development and Evaluation in Higher Education,* on the core committee of the Professional and Organizational Development Network, and on the program advisory committee for the International Conference on Improving University Teaching.

His books include *How Colleges Evaluate Professors* (1975), *Teaching Professors to Teach* (1977), *Successful Faculty Evaluation Programs* (1980), *Changing Practices in Faculty Evaluation* (1984), and *Coping with Faculty Stress* (1987, as editor), a Jossey-Bass sourcebook in the New Directions for Teaching and Learning series. He has contributed numerous articles on evaluation and development to such publications as the *New York Times* and *Change* magazine.

In addition to consulting, writing, and teaching a full schedule of classes, Seldin plays tennis, race walks in marathons, and grows organic vegetables. He and his wife, Pat, have one son and two daughters.

Evaluating and Developing Administrative Performance

⽨ 1 ⽥

Changing Expectations and Roles
of Academic Administrators

Administrators of higher education have been able to muddle through one institutional crisis after another by the brush-fire approach. Successive institutional crises have been treated as individual brush fires to be put out as they occur without resorting to comprehensive solutions. For many decades this piecemeal policy has worked.

During those decades, however, colleges and universities were serene institutions with few or none of the pressures of the bitterly competitive outside world. Presidents, provosts, deans, and department chairs were scholar-educators who saw themselves as first among equals. In this academic nirvana, administrative life on campus was marked by collegiality, expanding budgets, and a leisurely work pace. Many academic administrators found life so pleasant and comfortable that they stayed in their positions for a decade or more.

But the situation is very different today. Directing an institution of higher education now means facing a series of unrelenting demands. On many campuses, collegiality has been replaced by a "we" versus "they" mentality. Budgets are tight, the work pace has quickened. Computers are producing bewildering changes in the way things are done. Lawsuits are cropping up over a growing variety of real and imagined grievances. Government agencies are imposing restrictive rules and regula-

1

tions that the courts are enforcing. The demand for accountability has become a ground swell across the nation, and it has forced administrators to examine the cost-effectiveness of each program and each department, as well as the performance of each person. The tendency toward administrative specialization has accelerated as has a more businesslike approach. In short, the job of the academic administrator has become more complex, more pressured.

The "New Breed"

Today's academic administrator is expected to know how to handle budgetary and fiscal matters, to be able to deal with government agencies, courts, and trustees, and to be expert at collective bargaining and public relations. The administrator is also expected to shine in managerial skills, organizational strategy, budget analysis, and human relations. The new breed of academic administrator is variously referred to as a politician, a business executive, an orchestra conductor, a zoo keeper, a super entrepreneur, and a dispensing machine operator (Austin and Gamson, 1983).

Many administrators today dress in pinstripe suits, operate computers, and know their way around corporate offices and government agencies. They shake hands firmly and speak warmly, as if running for office. Plante (1985) is persuaded that their effectiveness as leaders is increasingly measured in the community by how often their pictures appear in newspapers and how often they are featured in "People to Watch." In the vernacular, they work hard at "pressing flesh" and "getting ink."

This new breed has adopted the style of business and public relations executives. As administrators, they manage by objectives, appoint marketing teams, and speak the jargon of the business world—cost-benefit analysis, market share, investment opportunity—with familiarity and ease. They have a sixth sense in dealing with newspaper editors, politicians, budget officers, alumni, and faculty leaders so that no matter what the problem, they land on their feet. Keller (1983, p. 56) writes, "They know that they are expected to pull a hat trick—to trim and find more economical ways of operating while actually raising quality further in the 1980s [1990s], to become better by becoming leaner."

In many institutions, the new management style represents much more than a shift in tone and manner. It represents belated recognition that institutions of higher education are something more than a collection of educators. These institutions are operating organizations that can benefit from the same management principles that guide profit-making corporations. Keller (1983, p. 59) finds that "more and more, academic leaders are beginning to sense that unless their campuses have some solid, active, rational management they may not make it through the next decade, or may not pass through the period without wounds and distentions."

A recent advertisement in the *Chronicle of Higher Education* for a college president lists these qualifications:

- Proven fiscal management, budget planning, successful employee relations, positive relations with minorities
- Strong organizational planning and leadership skills
- Superior communication skills and a regard for human interests and concerns
- The ability to represent effectively the institution's interests at all levels of government and within the business community
- The ability to raise funds for the institution by alternative financing methods
- Demonstrated skills in economic development, including work with business, industry, unions, government agencies, and Chambers of Commerce

Contrast the above array of presidential skills with those called for ten years ago by an institution similar in size, mission, location, and reputation:

Wanted: College president

- Experienced in administration
- Committed to faculty governance, student involvement, and cooperation with neighboring institutions

What caused the more demanding approach to academic administration? According to Keller (1983, p. 45), the approach "is being hammered out blow by blow under the duress of financial deficits, cutbacks, enrollment declines, and the demands of the paying clients. It is also being assembled in the less fiery areas of new courses, programs, and workshops for academic executives, coaxing them into new habits, introducing them to financial and strategic planning, performance controls, and collaborative decision making." Austin and Gamson (1983) cite such additional reasons as (1) more state and federal regulations, (2) more budgetary problems, and (3) more demands for accountability.

The Changing Face of Academic Administration

The new crop of presidents, provosts, deans, and department chairs is bringing a new management style to higher education. They are adapting all the tried and true elements from corporate management—especially from the nonprofit sector—and the state-of-the-art findings of organizational behavior, psychology, and administrative research.

What are the important components of this new style of administration? The following list was culled from a review of the current literature and additionally developed in discussion with many college and university administrators.

1. *Administrators are becoming more active.* They are now pointing the way, choosing priorities, constructing academic strategies, and providing active leadership. In the words of the provost of a large midwestern university: "The days of passive, laissez-faire management are over. Financial exigency has forced us to make selective cuts based on academic priorities and quality. Our involvement in managing the institution is far greater today than ever before."

In a prescient observation, Boulding (1975) wrote that "one of education's first priorities ... should be to develop a new generation of academic administrators who are skilled in the process of adjusting to decline" (p. 5). He added that "the skills of managing a declining institution are not only different from but in some sense greater than those required to manage institutional growth" (p. 8).

2. *Financial considerations are becoming more important.* Finances and academics are coming together. Today, departments and institutions routinely study the financial implications when they consider new academic programs. In the same way, financial officials consult faculty, deans, and provosts on the educational implications of contemplated financial decisions. No longer do academic administrators gear up programs or hire staff without cautious weighing of costs.

Most campus operations are largely nonacademic. These include housing, dining rooms and cafeterias, security, athletics, transportation, counseling and medical help, placement, purchasing, heating and cooling, endowment, record keeping, bookstores, maintenance, construction, and accounts receivable and payable. All these functions lend themselves beautifully to state-of-the-art business practices. To preserve money for the academic side, these nonacademic functions are getting extraordinary attention (Keller, 1983).

Since many administrators have skimpy backgrounds in financial planning and quality control, there is a pressing need for them to learn such skills. Generally, they do so by attending in-house or off-campus development programs (for details, see Chapter Seven).

3. *Technology is becoming a necessary tool for management.* As colleges and universities are buffeted by financial distress, the computer has become almost indispensable in dealing with forecasting, reallocation, financial planning, and retrenchment. In her study of five universities, Rubin (1977) found that a major reason for the expansion of information capacity was the institution's need to "cope with retrenchment, such as better projections of enrollment by department, better record keeping of expenditures and fund balances, and more data on credit-hour production by departments." Administrators facing retrenchment decisions needed more information because "they could not afford to make mistakes and they needed to justify their retrenchment decisions" (p. 247).

The new breed of academic administrators is computer

literate or at least capable of using computer calculations, and their offices often have terminals. Even those administrators who are unfamiliar with computer languages ask "what if" questions of their computer-literate staff: What if we have to make cuts in humanities programs? How much will we save if . . . ? (Keller, 1983).

Computers have earned a place for themselves far beyond their value in coping with retrenchment. The program manager of Academic Information Systems at IBM in New Milford, Connecticut, has suggested that information technology offers academic administrators three major opportunities:

1. It can enhance the efficiency of resource utilization and the results one gets as well as the general effectiveness of the educational organization.
2. It can strengthen the institution by creating all kinds of information that would take too much time to obtain by hand, if it could be obtained at all.
3. It can be the focal point for change or the excuse to change. There are often times when academic administrators know that they want to do something differently. But it is the technology that gives them the excuse to take some action (Mal Nechis, telephone interview, Oct. 1987).

Nechis, however, also pointed out the major challenge that must be considered when using information technology for administrative purposes: "From a managerial standpoint, educational institutions must meet the challenge of balancing the multiple alternatives and pressures that come up when you want to use the technology. . . . It is critically important to keep the focus on the institution's objectives and its strengths. Don't get diverted by the idea that if we only install this computer network we are going to be the best known school for having installed the network. That may be nice, but it may have nothing to do with institutional objectives and goals."

4. *Campus governance is being reshaped.* Keller (1983) notes that because academic administrators must move quickly and decisively yet continue to solicit faculty advice and guid-

ance, a new kind of governance is emerging on many campuses—the so-called Joint Big-Decisions Committee.

This committee usually is composed of several senior faculty members and key administrators and is bolstered at some sessions with a few junior faculty members, students, or trustees. It is usually chaired by the chief academic officer and has become the power center on many campuses. Essentially, the committee advises the president (or provost or dean) on what actions to take. At Ohio University, it is known as the University Planning Advisory Council. At the University of Michigan, it is the Budget and Priorities Committee. At Pace University (New York), it is the Dean's Advisory Council.

Although not resorting to a formal Joint Big-Decisions Committee, many colleges and universities have adopted the consultative approach to decision making. They bring in administrators, faculty, and students to advise on decisions that affect them. For effective participatory decisions, each participant must possess full information on the issues in a form that is both understandable and useful. Final decisions are still left to the academic administrators. But they are aided by a corps of advisers who develop ideas, draft position papers, and at the same time build support for the decision (Austin and Gamson, 1983).

Governance is also being reshaped in another area on many campuses. Unhappy with the quality of undergraduate education, many boards of trustees are assuming direct responsibility for academic decision making. Thus, the trustees' new assertiveness is redefining the hoary principle that they should act only as policy makers and overseers and not be involved in everyday academic affairs (Jacobson, 1985). Not surprisingly, this transformation frequently pits governing boards against academic administrators.

5. *Administrators are demonstrating new-found entrepreneurial skills.* On campus after campus, presidents, provosts, and deans are applying their skills to raise money, mobilize support for new initiatives, and supply a sense of direction for their institutions. Wielding the power to allocate resources among different institutional programs, they create incentives for class-

room experimentation, authorize the purchase of expensive equipment (such as computers), and recognize and reward professors who contribute the most to educational improvement (Bok, 1986).

The president of a midwestern college marveled at this new entrepreneurial approach: "It is really a question of seizing the initiative. Nothing like it existed in the past. Administrators are actively hunting for every opportunity for institutional growth and development. Anything from recruiting a prize-winning faculty member to investing a small fortune in an industrial park."

6. *Closer attention is now paid to the external environment, the market, and strategic planning.* There is today much more sensitivity to the economic, political, and cultural environment surrounding colleges and universities, as well as to the market for educational services. The higher education market has brought millions of adult learners to campuses, and these learners have triggered phenomenal growth in the fields of business, engineering, and computer science at the expense of home economics, social work, and foreign languages (Keller, 1983).

The external environment has lost much of its former casual and friendly support. Regulations are being imposed, appropriations are being slashed, and accountability is being raised almost as a war cry. The public is questioning whether what it is getting for its tuition dollars is actually worth the money.

Institutional planning is no longer the private domain of those who do not involve others in decision making but base planning essentially on hunch. The new breed of academic administrator has converted the process into a public event based on explicit objectives and rational strategies and supported by hard data. In the words of a western college provost: "We can't afford to engage in the haphazard, unrealistic planning of the past. The financial risk is simply too great. Our trustees insist on hard data. The slogan here is 'strategic analysis and planning.'"

7. *Evaluating and developing administrators is becoming more important.* If nothing else, today's academic administrator faces a host of challenges, and to meet them requires a fair measure of expertise in finance, governance, technology, communications, computers, and strategic planning.

How to ensure reasonable competency in these areas? At a growing number of institutions, close attention is now given to the administrator's abilities and productivity. Institutions recognize that without a generous infusion of funds the chief hope for improved campus management is to improve current administrative performance and to make every new appointment an outstanding one. Actually, by evaluating and developing administrative performance, institutions can effect positive change even if nothing else is done.

As Cheit (1975, p. 170) has remarked, "A new style is emerging on campus. Unlike the old one which sought improved quality mainly by adding income, the new one relies mainly on control, planning, evaluation . . . to provide institutional strength."

Evaluating and Improving Administrative Performance

Much too often, academics look upon appraisal of performance and professional development as unrelated processes. The fact is, they are a single process and make most sense as such. True, administrative evaluation can be helpful in making personnel decisions and in responding to external and internal pressures. But its core purpose is to locate areas of needed or desired improvement and to point the way to personal and professional development, which in turn enhances the institution's performance.

External and Internal Pressures. Informal assessment of performance is inevitable in any organization that must make hiring, promotion, salary, and dismissal decisions. Especially in periods of declining enrollment and economic uncertainty, these personnel decisions assume great importance. Thus, in recent years a more serious interest in administrative evaluation has developed. This contrasts with the general view held years ago that administrative evaluation served a useful, if dilettantish, purpose. Institutions can no longer afford to employ academic administrators who perform marginally. Evaluation helps to establish a reference base for personnel decisions.

Pressure to evaluate has come from both external and internal sources, including government, trustees, alumni, students, parents, taxpayers, and the general public. Pressure comes also from professors who argue that student evaluation of faculty should be paired with faculty evaluation of administrators, from administrators who insist on their right to be evaluated, and from institutions desirous of protecting their personnel decisions from successful legal challenges under antidiscrimination laws. In addition, those involved in higher education have become much more interested in such business practices as formal evaluation programs with established criteria, rating forms, and sources of information.

Enhancing Individual Performance. The primary reason to evaluate administrative performance systematically is to improve it. In a review of the literature, Nordvall (1979) suggests that this can be achieved by (1) providing a sharper, clearer definition of the administrator's role; (2) being more sensitive to the way that the administrator's performance is perceived by those who work directly with him or her; (3) helping the administrator plan career decisions; and (4) assessing administrative strengths and weaknesses to help guide professional and personal development.

Seldin (1987) adds another reason for administrative appraisal in that it will very likely prod senior-level managers (such as presidents and provosts) to be more watchful of their administrators and to coach and motivate them by providing feedback on their performance. The best rationale for administrative assessment is that it reinforces positive behavior and identifies areas of needed improvement.

Enhancing Institutional Performance. To elevate institutional functioning the institution must (1) improve internal communication and teamwork, (2) develop an inventory of personal resources for training or reassignment, (3) attract and retain top-quality administrators, (4) widen the personnel decision-making process to include staff participation, (5) develop information on how well institutional policies and administrative actions mesh, (6) provide data for research projects on factors influencing administrative effectiveness, and (7) determine if institutional goals are consistent with individual objectives.

While there is no hard evidence that improved administrative performance enhances student learning, it is likely that such performance does strengthen the overall operation of the institution and, as a result, helps it meet its educational goals.

Resistance to Administrator Evaluation. Even if the goals of administrative evaluation are pure and honorable, not everyone will embrace the process. Fisher (1987) finds that objections are directed not at the primary purpose of strengthening performance but rather at the potential side effects of the assessment process. Some opponents argue that the sheer diversity of leadership roles makes any system of assessment unworkable. Others scoff at assessment techniques as unproven. And still others think that behind every evaluation is a political agenda that inevitably makes the process highly subjective.

Farmer (1979) and Seldin (1987) offer several counterarguments to these objections: (1) flexibility can be introduced into the assessment process to offset diversity; (2) literally hundreds of colleges and universities have successfully used evaluation techniques; and (3) safeguards are available to protect against obtrusive subjectivity.

Checklist for Successful Evaluation Systems. The following checklist was developed from a review of the current literature on administrative evaluation and from discussions with more than 100 deans, provosts, and presidents throughout the country:

1. Formal, objective standards must replace personal values and biases in judging administrative performance.
2. The appraisal process must not be overly long.
3. Ratings from multiple sources must be obtained.
4. Each source of information must have firsthand knowledge of the administrator's performance.
5. Specific, criteria-based means of assessing performance must be employed.
6. Appraisals must provide adequate information about the subtleties and nuances of managerial performance.
7. An appraisal must be viewed as a fragile, sensitive process that involves both people and data.
8. Administrators must know the kind of performance expected of them.

9.   Senior administrators must be willing to confront mediocre subordinates with realistic ratings.
10. Frequent performance feedback must be given. Where appropriate, it should be accompanied by specific suggestions for improvement.
11. Senior administrators must conduct appraisal interviews so that they result in motivation, not demoralization, of subordinates.
12. A person conducting an appraisal interview should play the role of teacher and coach rather than that of judge.
13. The process and procedures employed to assess an administrator on one level may be inappropriate for assessing an administrator on a different level.
14. The evaluation procedures must be designed painstakingly. They must fit the mode of operation and style of the institution.

Developing Administrative Performance. Whereas the primary purpose of assessment is to recognize strengths and locate areas in need of improvement, the primary purpose of development is to help meet those needs in a compatible framework of individual and institutional goals. Out of a broad spectrum of professional growth opportunities, the appraisal results help individual improvement plans to take shape (Fisher, 1987).

Academic administrators are still selected primarily for their scholarly qualifications rather than for their administrative experience—of which they often have little. This is true not only in the United States but also in most other countries (Hughes, 1987). Most department chairs, deans, provosts, and presidents arrive at their posts by moving through the academic ranks, picking up administrative skills as they go along.

In recent years, however, the new breed of administrator has been unwilling to rely on on-the-job training as the *sole* way to acquire management and leadership skills. The new breed does not denigrate personal experience, not at all. But he recognizes that such fragmented experience does not by itself provide adequate preparation for the numerous and weighty responsibilities of an administrator. Relying exclusively on one's personal experience means that one loses the benefit of others' experience, and such reliance is apt to be costly, both financially and otherwise, in judgmental errors made in pursuit of experience.

So the new breed enhances on-the-job training by participating in seminars, workshops, and institutes to gain an accelerated understanding of the art and science of administration. In addition, the new breed takes part in administrative internships and campuswide administrative development programs (Fisher, 1987).

Several organizations are today filling the demand for management skills in academia. For example, the American Association of State Colleges and Universities in Washington, D.C., has a Resource Center for Planned Change, which stresses recognition of social, economic, legal, and technological trends to respond to, get a jump on, or defend against (Keller, 1983). The American Council on Education, also in Washington, offers many programs for deans, academic vice-presidents, and presidents in such areas as financial planning, law, and quality assessment and control. The National Center for Higher Education Management Services in Boulder, Colorado, gives management seminars on strategic planning, analyzing costs for resource allocation, financial management, and assessing institutional effectiveness.

Some colleges and universities offer on-campus seminars to train academic administrators in marketing, financial planning, communications, computer modeling, strategic decision making, data collection and management, and performance appraisal. Harvard University, Carnegie Mellon University (Pittsburgh), the University of Texas, and Wichita State University are among the institutions that have developed such in-house programs.

Several researchers (Toombs and Marlier, 1981; Austin and Gamson, 1983; Schulman, 1983; Seldin, 1987) have recommended another approach to development. They suggest innovative rearrangements of work loads to stimulate faculty growth. Moreover, if an adaptation works for faculty, it should also work for administrators. What is recommended here are (1) in-house lectureship programs in which senior administrators act as resources for less experienced administrators; (2) brief teach-

ing assignments, particularly on the graduate level, to help administrators expand their knowledge; (3) summer or year-long
internships in government or industry; and (4) exchange programs with both academic and nonacademic institutions.

There are still other approaches. The one finally selected
to sharpen the skills of an administrator will depend on such
factors as his or her position, type of institution, motivation of
the individual, and available time and funds. However, certain
desirable features of an administrator development program
turn up repeatedly on lists compiled by Lindquist (1978), Nordvall (1979), Murphy (1984), and Seldin (1987):

1. At the outset, recognize that there is no single best style
   of administrative behavior.
2. Whatever program is selected, it should be a natural outgrowth of the administrator's evaluation.
3. The program should be tailored to and reflect the needs of
   both the individual and the institution.
4. Participation in the program should be voluntary.
5. The program should have clearly defined goals and modest
   expectations.
6. The program should be supportive, certainly nonthreatening.
7. Where applicable, the program should focus not only on
   the individual administrator but also on the administrative
   team.
8. Confidences should not be breached.
9. The program should concentrate on the more important
   of the many roles of the administrator.
10. The program should recognize the stage of the administra-
    tor's life and career.

To say that the precise management and leadership skills
required to deal with the administrative challenges facing higher education are in dispute is to state a truism. The argument
over whether a scholar or a manager makes the more effective
administrator will endure for as long as there are a chicken and an
egg. However, the adversaries close ranks in agreeing that an ad-

ministrator is an important human resource whose talents, sensibilities, and skills can and should be carefully cultivated (Gaff, Festa, and Gaff, 1978; Seldin, 1983).

Academic Culture

Successful administration is an outgrowth not only of the administrator's skills in combination with the strategy, structure, and reward system of the institution. It also has something to do with the style, the character, or the way of doing things that stamps the institution itself. At the risk of becoming metaphysical, let us say that this invisible quality is the institutional equivalent of the human soul. For want of a better designation, let us call it the academic culture.

This culture is the unspoken language that conveys to administrators what is important and what is not important, as well as how they are expected to behave and do things. Loosely defined, academic culture is the amalgam of beliefs, mythology, values, and esprit that sets one institution apart from another, that acts as a kind of institutional fingerprint.

A number of researchers have examined academic culture in various institutions in an attempt to reveal its anatomy. The following list of characteristics has been adapted from Seldin (1986), Schuster (1985), and Robbins (1984), as well as from experience:

1. *Individual autonomy.* How much responsibility, independence, and opportunity are given to administrators in the institution?
2. *Identification.* How much and in which areas do academic administrators (chairs and deans, for example) identify with the institution rather than with their departments or schools?
3. *Personnel.* To what extent do administrators and faculty have confidence in the integrity and competency of each other?
4. *Conflict tolerance.* How much conflict exists among administrators? Between administrators and faculty? How

willing are both groups to be open and candid about the conflicts?

5. *Cooperation.* How well do the institution's personnel work toward shared goals and objectives?

6. *Decision making.* How much consultation and collaboration go into the decision-making process? Does "participation" simply mean lip service?

7. *Support.* How much warmth and support are provided by senior administrators to subordinates?

8. *Communication.* Does complete, accurate, and meaningful information flow upward, downward, and across the institution? How often and under what circumstances?

9. *Sense of community.* To what extent do members of the institution feel a sense of togetherness? A sense of genuine sharing and caring about each other?

10. *Risk tolerance.* Are administrators encouraged to be professionally adventuresome, innovative, and willing to take risks? How often and when?

11. *Inner satisfaction.* Do administrators take from their work a sense of achievement, pride in a job well done, and a feeling of competency, personal growth, and development?

12. *Rewards.* Are performance rewards—salary increase, promotion—based on meaningful criteria, standards, and evidence?

Each of these twelve areas is a continuum along which academic culture can be glimpsed and estimated. Taken together, they paint a reasonably accurate portrait of the institution.

Much of an institution's academic culture is communicated, sometimes openly and sometimes silently, by the institution's senior administrators. The president, executive vice-president, provost, and dean suggest pointedly by their own behavior the administrative values and behaviors expected of all personnel. Consider the following examples:

• A Minnesota college president demonstrated the kind of ingenuity and dedication expected of the staff by using a snowmobile to get to work.

- A new dean of the Harvard Business School indicated his belief that families come ahead of careers by declining to work weekends.
- The president's office at the University of Pennsylvania set up a fund to reimburse faculty members for entertaining student groups in their homes or in local restaurants.
- The chancellor of Pace University reminded the staff to go out of its way to help students, to welcome them, and to deal with them courteously.
- Senior administrators at Haverford College (Pennsylvania) conduct exit interviews with graduating students and ask questions such as, "Did Haverford live up to your expectations?"

Academic culture sometimes exerts a positive or negative bias on administrative evaluation. It can be positive when deeply shared beliefs facilitate communication and generate unstinting cooperation and commitment. But it can be negative when the shared beliefs and values are out of step with the needs of the institution, its members, and its other constituencies (Sathe, 1983).

An examination of certain basic processes at the heart of any institution will provide a closer look at the influence academic culture has on performance evaluation.

1. *Communication.* Implicit in an institution's beliefs and values is the decision as to how openly to communicate details about an evaluation program. Many institutions provide an A to Z rundown on their evaluation programs, explaining everything candidly and completely. Their cultures place high store on open communication, and their objective is for every administrator to be well informed about the programs. Other institutions operating in different cultures are more secretive, noncommittal, and parsimonious with pertinent details, both when explaining and when implementing the program.

2. *Top-down or bottom-up administration.* When the prevailing management style is top down, major decisions are made and details are worked out by a few senior administrators with scant consultation with others. A ready-to-use evaluation program is simply announced by the president or provost and

then promptly implemented. When the management style is
bottom up, the personnel to be evaluated actively participate in
developing and implementing the program. In a sense, they
"own" the program because they share in the control of their
own futures.

3. *Trust versus suspicion.* Some academic cultures are
marked by a high level of mutual trust and respect among the
institution's staff. The normal discomfort felt by those facing
evaluation is handled sensitively and reassuringly. The result is
that the discomfort tends to melt away. In contrast, academic
cultures that are rife with suspicion and resist the evaluation
program may witness the handling of suspicion and resistance
by a dose of muscle power.

4. *Performance appraisal.* Some academic cultures view
performance appraisal as a negative, even punitive, activity.
They stubbornly hold to the belief that the hidden purpose of
the appraisal is to gather evidence to "get" someone. Not surprisingly, administrators in these cultures tend to back away
from procedures designed to evaluate their performance. In other cultures, administrators recognize that the purpose of appraisal is to improve performance. They have little hesitation in
embracing the program.

5. *Teamwork.* On some campuses, the senior administrators, middle-level administrators, faculty, and staff are considered to be separate units, each doing a job in relative isolation
from the other units. This prevents them from thinking like a
team with a common purpose. Performance is often evaluated
only by immediate superiors because it is thought that others in
the institution are not in a position to judge. On other campuses,
superiors, subordinates, faculty, and staff are generally ready to
join in evaluating an administrator's performance.

6. *Leadership at the top.* In some academic cultures, the
president offers the kind of lukewarm support of the evaluation
program that is transparently negative. By not providing enough
resources, not breaking procedural impasses, and not giving
vocal support to the program, the president unmistakenly communicates silent opposition. In other academic cultures, the
president actively mobilizes campus support, provides adequate

resources, comes up with compromise suggestions to break log-jams, and readily agrees to evaluation of his or her own performance. The message of support is read clearly by everyone.

7. *Caliber of work.* At some institutions, the performance level of administrators and faculty is acceptable though nondescript. No one really regrets the absence of a well-functioning evaluation program aimed at improving performance. At other institutions, the administrators and faculty are expected to perform in top gear and anything less is not tolerated. The institutional demand for distinguished performance is met by the administrators and faculty. The evaluation program is fine tuned to encourage and reward steady improvement.

8. *Cultural network.* There are informal and invisible communication lines in every college and university. This network consists of individuals who spread the lore that reinforces the institution's core values. In some academic cultures, however, the network is flaccid, and the individuals operating it are relatively undistinguished. The result is a campus that is fertile with rumors and anxieties and that offers a poor environment in which to conduct administrative evaluations. But in other academic cultures, the network is sturdy, and those spreading the gospel are distinguished leaders in their fields. Administrative evaluations in such cases are conducted in an accepting, welcoming environment.

9. *Importance of evidence.* Some academic cultures encourage their members to form opinions and make decisions primarily on the basis of gut feelings and hunches. The information collection process is a casual one and may at times consist of nothing more than informal conversations. Other academic cultures operate with more rigorous standards and require multiple sources of information, firsthand knowledge, fairness, and thoroughness in administrative appraisals.

Conclusion

There is no "best" way for colleges and universities to evaluate and develop their academic administrators. The selected method will depend in large measure on the characteristics of the academic culture of the institution. Subsequent chapters will present many questions to be considered when constructing a performance evaluation for administrators. A few examples follow:

1. What level is the administrative position? President? Academic vice-president? Provost? Dean? Chair?
2. Why is the evaluation being conducted? For a personnel decision? Performance improvement?
3. How should performance be assessed? By structured or unstructured narrative? Documentation?
4. Who should assess it? Supervisor? Peers? Faculty? Subordinates? Clients served? Self?
5. How often should performance be evaluated? Every six months? One year? Three years? Five years?
6. How much money and time should be assigned to this evaluation?

Similarly, questions addressing the administrator's professional development will also be answered largely through consideration of the institution's academic culture. For example:

1. What is the administrator's rank?
2. What specific areas need improvement?
3. What do campus administrators think about the concept of professional development?
4. How much financial support is available for development programs?
5. What are the time constraints?
6. What is the administrator's motivation to strengthen performance?
7. Which approach or combination of approaches to professional development is likely to be most successful for this administrator? Discussion? Training sessions that concentrate on specific skills? Altered reward system? Growth contract? Reading? Mentoring? Conferences? Internship? Outward Bound training?

This chapter has explored the new breed of academic administrators, the assessment and development of their performance, and the academic cultures that serve as backdrops for their institutional evaluation and development.

The next chapter will examine the principles, benefits, and pitfalls of assessing administrative performance.

⊁ 2 ⊀

Why Assess
Administrative Performance?

Informal evaluation of administrative performance has long been practiced in academic institutions. In fact, this kind of evaluation is probably as old as the institutions themselves. Much of it is the result of casual observation. Faculty members pick up impressions of an administrator's competency and swap these impressions with professional peers. Students form opinions about administrative effectiveness after encounters with administrative staff. Even administrators gain fragmentary impressions about fellow administrators and give voice to their impressions. In short, a campus has many individuals who harbor casual opinions of the quality of the work of others and share these opinions with friends or colleagues.

What is new, however, is the attempt to root out hearsay and gossip—the hoary communicative channels of organizations—in favor of more open, factual, and systematic evaluation of administrative performance.

Today's increased interest in appraising administrative performance grows out of the demand for more accountability in every sector of the academic community. This demand has been made by government agencies, trustees, alumni, and the general public. What is more, the demand has been fueled by three additional factors: (1) the contention by faculty members that their evaluation must be matched by evaluation of adminis-

22

trators, (2) the growing need to shelter personnel decisions from successful legal challenge under antidiscrimination as well as other laws, and (3) the acceptance by more colleges and universities of management principles that place high store on evaluation of performance, goal setting, and periodic feedback.

The research literature reflects this remarkable movement toward administrative evaluation. Consider a few examples. In a 1973 survey of 218 institutional members of the American Association of State Colleges and Universities, Surwill and Heywood (1976) found that only 17 percent of the institutions conducted formal evaluations of their academic deans. A few years later, however, Baum (1979) expressed his belief that the number of institutions adopting or on the threshold of adopting a formalized evaluation procedure for administrators had multiplied. Miller (1979) concurred, saying that formalized administrative evaluation was casting a bigger shadow on the collegiate landscape. Baum's and Miller's perceptions were validated in 1986 when Lynch, Bowker, and McFerron reported to the American Educational Research Association that of 371 chief liberal arts academic officers surveyed, some 66 percent acknowledged that their administrative performance had been formally evaluated.

The burgeoning of administrative evaluation is also reflected in the following cases as reported in the *Chronicle of Higher Education:*

- A Minnesota judge ruled that a local newspaper could have access to a portion of a consultant's evaluation of C. Peter Magrath, the outgoing president of the University of Minnesota ("Minn. Judge Releases . . . ," 1984).
- The trustees of Colorado Mountain College, arguing that the institution was in need of new leadership, announced that they would not renew the president's contract ("Colorado Mountain College Fires . . . ," 1986).
- The trustees of the California State University System voted to evaluate the job performance of the presidents of the system's nineteen campuses every five years ("Five-Year Evaluations Planned . . . ," 1983).

• Several trustees of the California State University System
  criticized the chancellor's performance for, among other
  things, her "unconscionable and unprofessional" handling of
  a review of the evaluation of the president of one of the
  campuses (McCurdy, 1987).

A recent article in the *New York Times* reported on the
evaluation of the administration at George Mason University by
the faculty senate. Significantly, the chairman of the senate
commented that, while the president did a fine job representing
the institution to off-campus groups, he was unable to deal effectively with the campus community ("Mason University:
Twenty-Nine, Growing Fast," 1986).

Why Evaluate Administrator Performance?

There are three important reasons to evaluate college
and university administrators: (1) to improve their performance, (2) to provide a rational and equitable basis for personnel decisions, and (3) to anticipate and be able to respond to
demands to assess performance.

Evaluation to Improve Performance. There is no better
reason to evaluate than to improve performance. Evaluation
provides data with which to assist the faltering, to motivate the
tired, and to encourage the indecisive. Administrators are hired
by institutions in expectation of first-class performance. To
help administrators hone their performance is nothing more
than a logical extension of this expectation. Just as students and
faculty need feedback and guidance to correct errors, so administrators require helpful direction if they are to improve their
performance.

To achieve measurable improvement, however, the administrator must accept the evaluative process and have the capacity to make the necessary changes. Simply handing over the
results of an evaluation is unlikely to motivate the administrator
to make significant changes. That result is more likely if the administrator reviews the evaluation with an immediate superior.
Aside from congratulations or sympathy, what should come out

of the review are specific suggestions on how to improve performance. Many colleges and universities provide on-site training or send administrators to outside workshops or seminars to shore up weaknesses, develop strengths, and catch up on recent professional developments. A basic test of the willingness of a college or university to help administrators improve performance is its provision of support, both psychological and financial.

An effective evaluation of performance should not be restricted to one or two administrative functions. It should include a wide range of such functions. Depending on the position of the person being evaluated, it might include planning, decision making, ability to deal with people, communication skills, initiative, adaptability, problem-solving skills, and leadership.

Whether it is to improve performance or to make personnel decisions, the process employed in administrator evaluation is the same. The steps include gathering detailed data from many sources, joint analysis of the data by the administrator and his or her superior, isolating and identifying the skills requiring improvement, and planning and implementing corrective action. Confidentiality of the data must be guarded throughout the entire evaluation process. Dissemination of the results must have the explicit consent of the administrator and be at his or her discretion. Data gathered for the ostensible purpose of improving performance must not be used for personnel decisions. Should this rule be abused, it may have a chilling, even fatal, impact on the institution's entire evaluation program.

Evaluation for Personnel Decisions. To provide a rational and equitable basis for promotion and retention decisions is another reason for assessing administrative performance. Such decisions have of course always been made by colleges and universities, but the circumstances surrounding them are changing. In recent years, under growing public demand for accountability, more institutions have moved personnel decisions to the top of the list of reasons for assessing administrative performance. With salaries plus benefits for deans, vice-presidents, and presidents typically ranging from $50,000 to $125,000, personnel decisions to promote or retain top-level administrators can have significant financial implications.

In their pursuit of sound personnel decisions, however, many institutions have stumbled in setting up evaluation programs. Inaccurate data-gathering procedures have contaminated the programs and led to flawed decisions. Practices on many campuses are marred by a get-it-done-quickly approach to evaluation. As the head of the faculty senate at a midwestern college commented, "The president wanted feedback from the faculty on the academic vice-president's performance, and he wanted it, in any form we wanted to give it, within seven days."

Administrators are in general agreement that deadwood needs pruning from the staff. But they balk at what they consider a subjective screening process, especially one conducted in haste. As Eble (1978, p. 122) cautions, "Administrators' performances need to be evaluated in systematic ways. . . . Serving purely at the pleasure of the administrative hierarchy and being subject to no more scrutiny than the offhand one of a higher-ranking administrator are ill-advised practices."

Evaluation to Provide Data to Outsiders. Another compelling reason to assess administrative performance is to be able to provide data to persons and organizations operating off campus. Government officials, parents, taxpayers, boards of trustees, alumni, the general public, and a considerable number of advocacy groups constantly request all sorts of data bearing on the institution's operation. In fact, a number of state legislatures now require colleges and universities to maintain records on the hiring, retention, and promotion of faculty and administrators.

Few doubts remain today that evaluation is an important tool in the administration of colleges and universities. The voices favoring evaluation include off-campus individuals and organizations, along with researchers and writers such as Dressel (1976), Eble (1978), Baum (1979), Llgen and Barnes-Farrell (1984), Miller (1985), Lynch, Bowker, and McFerron (1986), and Seldin (1987).

Pressure has also come in recent years from the implementation of many statewide assessment programs. Marchese (1985) reports that a primary objective of such programs is to measure either the performance of an institution or some of its programs. Since a frequent complaint of faculty members, especially during years of financial distress, is that their institutions are overloaded with highly paid administrators (Palmer, 1983), staffing patterns are being more closely scrutinized in many states as part of ongoing assessment programs. Institutions are being pressed to justify their staffing patterns, and justifications have to eschew the rhetorical for the factual. As a means of saving costs, for example, Oakland Community College (Michigan) increased the number of nonacademic clerical and support staff and significantly reduced the number of campus administrators (Nichols and Stuart, 1983).

To demonstrate a cause-and-effect relationship between administrative performance and student learning would obviously be gratifying, but it is patently beyond the reach of evidence. However, other benefits are demonstrable. Genova and others (1976), therefore, have concluded that an effective evaluation program is a requisite today on college and university campuses.

Operating Principles

Experience warns that when top-level administrators announce their intention to develop an appraisal program, the initial reaction is likely to be negative. Objections are voiced by many of the individuals whose performance will be appraised. Some of the negative response may be justified if parts of the evaluation program are fuzzy. Lahti (1978) says that too many programs overlook the epigram: "It is not whether you win or lose but how you play the game" (p. 1). Sharp differences of opinion may arise over a definition of performance. *Which* kinds of performance should be appraised? *How* should the evaluation be conducted? *Who* should participate? Considering the paucity of results, some evaluation programs are not worth the setup efforts. Lahti also reminds us that the plea for more humanism in assessment programs points up the need to consider not only the results of performance but also *how* the results were achieved. All in all, however, administrators must find inescapable the conclusion that appraisal is here to stay and that more is to be gained by everyone from a systematized appraisal program than from a catch-as-catch-can approach.

The development of any systematic method for appraising administrators is a time-consuming and complex process. It must also be recognized that the state of the art of administrator evaluation is about where faculty evaluation was a decade ago. The demand for improvement in evaluation programs is getting louder. No one seriously believes, however, that improvement in administrator evaluation will cure all the ills of colleges and universities. Evaluation is a tool for the collection of information, no more, no less. It is not an end in itself. Human judgment determines whether the information is used correctly or incorrectly. Misused, evaluation can be destructive. Used properly, it can be an instrument of change. It can serve as one of the many tools for institutional vitality, even survival.

Because colleges and universities differ widely and serve different constituencies, Genova and others (1976) suggest that an effective administrator evaluation program should follow certain operating principles:

- *Multipurpose.* Given the differences in institutional purposes and missions, the evaluation program should be tailored to the needs of the administrators being evaluated, their constituencies, and the institution as a whole.
- *Multifaceted.* To be fair and complete, the evaluation should encompass a wide range of activities and responsibilities, weighted according to importance.
- *Multisource.* To obtain a more accurate picture of the total administrator, evaluators should use a wide range of sources for data.
- *Multimethods.* Since administrative styles vary, different methods of assessment are needed. Though some processes of administration can be generalized across the board (such as communications adequacy), other processes are role specific (such as program budgeting).
- *The institution's frame of reference.* The institution's purpose, needs, history, scope, and stage of development should be the backdrop for, and give special meaning to, the assessment of particular administrative actions.

Based as they are on current research literature and years of practical experience, the following guidelines can be extremely helpful in developing a successful administrator evaluation program:

1. The program must be presented in a candid, complete, and clear way to every administrator. Any sugarcoating or obfuscation, in the explanatory process or in the implementation of the program, may doom it from the start. The goal is for the entire administrative staff to know—clearly, accurately, and completely—the precise requirements and evidentiary data utilized for decisions about retention, salary increases, and promotion. There must also be complete and accurate knowledge of institutional policies and practices in evaluating performance.

2. The administrators must have a significant hand in both the development and the operation of the evaluation program. They must sense that they are in control of their destiny. It may be necessary to develop separate standards for department chairs, deans, vice-presidents, and the president, but for fairness and accuracy these standards must be reviewed by a supervisory body, perhaps the board of trustees. The advantage of getting administrators to participate actively in the development of the evaluation program is that they will "own" the program. They will then more readily accept its implementation. And they will be more likely to consider the end product fair and meaningful.

3. The primary purpose of the evaluation procedure should be to improve the quality of the administration, and its approach should be positive rather than punitive. The procedure should be based on the belief that each administrator possesses different abilities and skills. The effort should be on maintaining the strengths and shoring up the weaknesses of administrators.

4. Top-level administrators must give their active support to evaluation policies and practices. They must be publicly committed to the program and see that it operates effectively. In addition, they must provide whatever resources are necessary to the program. The key administrator is usually the president. It is his or her role to break logjams, to come up with acceptable

compromises, and to lend the force of the presidential office to publicize the program on campus.

5. The evaluation program must take into account the tendency that academic administrators share with most human beings to regard evaluation as an implicit threat. It serves only to aggravate the problem to apply presidential muscle power to the resistance. Experience has provided more productive approaches. First, consider the evaluation program as experimental. Neither the procedures nor the instruments should be seen as etched in stone. Second, allow sufficient time—one or two years—for the process of acceptance and implementation. Use the time to draft, discuss, and modify procedures and documents. Third, keep moving forward. Don't allow the program to stall in a futile search for perfection. Fourth, start the program incrementally and apply pressure on resistance points in a civil, even compassionate, way; try to understand the reasons for the resistance and to come up with realistic ways to overcome it.

6. All administrators must know the performance standards by which they will be evaluated. Specifically, they must know what constitutes exemplary, satisfactory, and unsatisfactory performance. Additionally, they must know what criteria and weights will be used for their evaluation. Should the administrator fall short of the fixed standards, that failure should be discussed with him or her far in advance of a termination decision. The administrator should be given every opportunity to grow in ways that will benefit both the individual and the institution (Seldin, 1980b).

7. Policies and practices governing administrator evaluation must be in full accordance with civil rights legislation and affirmative action clauses. In today's legal environment, few institutions have been lucky enough to escape lawsuits initiated by aggrieved administrators who charge that they have been denied promotion or contract renewal for discriminatory reasons. Many evaluation programs have also been challenged in court as inadequate or biased. Certain data-gathering methods have been found wanting and, in some court decisions, illegal. It is no more than prudent for colleges and universities to reexamine

closely their administrative evaluation programs to eliminate inadequacies before a court orders them to do so.

8. It is wise to allow room for individual differences in the development of evaluation criteria, as long as these differences can be tolerated by the institution. Styles of governance differ. So do administrative responsibilities. The criteria used to evaluate the performance of an academic dean will be somewhat different from those used to evaluate a president. Many colleges and universities center attention, unfortunately, on the fine points of methodology rather than on criteria. They may spend more time deciding whether the evaluation should be scheduled for March or November than discussing what should be assessed. More important than *when* is *what* is to be evaluated.

9. The evaluation instruments must provide reliable and valid data at the proper technical level. The program must be careful to eliminate such critical defects as an irregular rating schedule, bias resulting from flawed instructions, and inconsistent or inadequate standards (Seldin, 1984).

10. The evaluation program must be firmly rooted in the traditions, purposes, and academic culture of the particular college or university. Policies and procedures that work well in one institution may falter or fail in another. The institution considering the introduction of an evaluation program would be wise to adapt a program operating in another institution and tailor it to fit local needs, politics, traditions.

11. To survive, the evaluation system must be accepted by those who evaluate and those who are evaluated. Individuals who do not endorse the system, or do so reluctantly, are unlikely to spend the time and effort to respond thoughtfully and meaningfully when asked to supply assessment data. Nor are administrators likely to respond with any enthusiasm to performance feedback when they perceive their evaluations as less than fair and accurate. Thus, a periodic assessment of the entire evaluation program is necessary as a basic safeguard (Llgen and Barnes-Farrell, 1984).

12. The cost of maintaining and implementing an evalua-

tion program must be weighed from time to time against the benefits of the program. Mondy and Noe (1984) point out that just getting a system started adds up to many hours of developmental costs. Also, the time involved in completing appraisal forms, maintaining appropriate records, conducting the evaluation interviews, and working with administrators on developmental activities is considerable. But the benefits of an effective evaluation program will far outweigh its costs. Promotion and compensation decisions are made easier because they rest on documented job performance. Best of all, the rising performance level of campus administrators benefits the institution and the administrators themselves.

13. The evaluation system must recognize the responsibilities and obligations of each administrator and any special circumstances or conditions in effect when he or she was hired. Also, says Dressel (1976), the system must consider: (1) the expectations and views of the different constituencies served by the institution; (2) the administrator's perception of his or her assigned tasks and responsibilities and the measure of success in achieving them; (3) the goals of the institution; (4) the extent to which the freedom of the administrator to act is limited by traditions, regulations, or lack of support from superiors in the hierarchy; and (5) the fact that the spectrum of administrative philosophy and style is very wide.

14. The program must include "upward" evaluation so that faculty members who have worked with administrators can participate in evaluating their performance. Seldin (1987) points out that this tends to improve managerial competency and nourish mutual understanding—both of which contribute to the institution's goals. A former chancellor of the State University of New York asserts that evaluation of administrators by faculty is nothing more than creative management and, further, that the very survival of the university in the United States depends on making administrators accountable in a way that is satisfactory to constituencies both within and outside the university (Boyer, 1974).

15. The program must avoid the common mistake of accepting the assessment of a single source, such as the administra-

tor's immediate supervisor, as representing the complete evaluation of the administrator. To do so is to ignore the multiple responsibilities of the administrator, as well as those aspects of the administrator's performance of which the supervisor may be unaware. Relying on a single source of information carries other risks. An individual judgment uncorrected by others may rest on a wrong assumption, faculty misinformation, or a fact colored by emotion. It is imperative to obtain multisource information to avoid arriving at a cardboard figure of the administrator. Superiors, subordinates, faculty, students, alumni, administrative peers, and the person being evaluated all provide potentially important but limited insights. No single strand is strong enough to stand alone. Truth is not simple. To get at it requires all the help one can muster.

16. The evaluation system must avoid the trap of trying to separate performance evaluation from the reward structure in an effort to avoid the "taint" of money issues from the assessment and feedback/counseling process. The two are so naturally intertwined as to defy separation. Why try? Lawler (1981) reports that most administrators believe rewards *should* be tied to performance. The connection is logical. Break the connection and one risks that administrators will shrug off their evaluation with the comment, "Why bother improving performance when it will have no bearing on my next salary increase?" Even a basic understanding of motivation and learning theory suggests that desirable behavior should be reinforced. Compensation has certainly proved its worth as a reinforcement instrument.

17. The evaluation system should be based on the idea that the purpose of gathering quantified, objective data is to help shape a subjective decision. Similarly, contract renewal and promotion decisions should be based on objective data, although the decisions themselves may be subjective. The data form the conduit for the judgment, the means to an end. Caution must be exercised about the extent of human judgment in the system, since human judgment divorced from objective data may be an invitation to tyranny. Seldin (1980b) comments that perhaps the best system is one that blends objective data into subjective judgment.

Deficiencies in Appraisal Programs and Cautions in Their Use

The philosopher Santayana warns that those who do not learn from their mistakes are doomed to repeat them. Colleges and universities, having decided to embark on administrative evaluation programs or to develop existing programs, can avoid many mistakes by learning from the experience of other institutions. There is no virtue in repeating errors.

Based on his review of the literature, Lahti (1978) has come up with certain deficiencies that are common in appraisal programs:

- Inadequate data on the subtleties of managerial performance
- Inconsistent ratings by individuals in different units in the same institution
- Excessive time demanded of individuals involved in the evaluation process
- Resistance to the rating system because of its perceived inability to make fair judgments or because the system is seen as defective
- An unwillingness to confront less effective subordinates with realistic ratings
- A delay in feedback to subordinates, thereby delaying effective reinforcement
- Vague criteria for administrative judgments, leaving individuals in the dark about the performance expected of them
- Negative feedback delivered without skill, leaving subordinates demoralized
- Unfair evaluations of good administrators
- Institutional failure to pay enough attention to staff development programs, expecting the evaluation process by itself to solve performance problems

Genova and others (1976) view as a major deficiency of some evaluation programs the institution's failure to be sure that it has a clear and compelling reason to embark on the program. In the rush to act, the institution can, and often does, unwittingly pay scant attention to specific aspects of the program and thus leaves a trail of misunderstandings, frustrations, and resentments. This is a perfect way to doom a fledgling program. It may save time and effort in the short run, but it has a heavy price tag in the long run. To correct mistakes and erase their stain from the minds of administrators is a long process, and some of the stain may turn out to be indelible.

Seldin (1987) cites additional deficiencies in many administrator evaluation programs:

- Administrators expected to turn in perfect performances in every area
- Programs not rooted in the traditions, goals, and style of the institution
- Performance not compared to the preagreed standards
- Confidentiality of results not maintained and distribution of results not controlled
- Denying administrators the opportunity to suggest the procedures or process to be used in their assessment
- The entire administrative assessment based on information from the immediate superior
- The entire administrative assessment based on one or two areas of responsibility
- Assessment criteria and procedures not clear or unilaterally selected
- Top-level administrators omitted from the evaluation program
- Insufficient time allowed for implementation of the program
- Lack of current and specific job descriptions
- Excessive cost in time and energy
- Evaluation policies and/or procedures that violate civil rights guidelines

A number of academics flatly oppose administrative evaluation and, according to Farmer (1979), base their opposition on three fundamental arguments:

1. The bewildering diversity of programs, leadership roles, and opinions on evaluation renders evaluation programs unworkable.
2. No techniques have proved to be really satisfactory.
3. The evaluation program inevitably disintegrates into a political process in which subjectivity overwhelms objectivity.

Farmer deals with these objections by arguing that (1) diversity can be accommodated without harming the workability of the program, (2) a number of evaluative techniques have already proved to be effective in higher education, and (3) many evaluation programs operating successfully on campuses today have built-in safeguards against subjectivity.

Nordvall (1979) expresses concern over the pockets of stubborn opposition on campuses to administrative evaluation programs, even though convincing counterarguments can be made that should reduce the opposition. The pockets of resistance persist, however, and can seriously hamper the assessment process.

As if these problems were not complex and numerous enough, Dressel (1976) comes up with additional ones. He asks for an exact definition of what administration is in relation to leadership and management. He wants to know exactly how much autonomy an administrator possesses, considering the organizational hierarchy and internal and external sources of authority. He also calls for clearer and more widely acceptable criteria for determining the degree of success of administrators.

The American Association of State Colleges and Universities (1976, p. 12) voices its own set of precautions:

• Avoid developing evaluation instruments for implementation during a crisis.
• Avoid evaluation instruments issued by special-interest groups.
• Avoid evaluations by individuals not competent to make them.
• Avoid the mass distribution of findings.

- Avoid accepting evaluation as a power play in collective bargaining.
- Avoid overstressing individual items apart from the context of the whole evaluation instrument.
- Avoid assigning the same value to different evaluations—examine the background of each respondent.
- Avoid making final recommendations based on evaluation materials that only represent a part of the total picture.

Miller (1985) comes up with a checklist of questions to be asked when evaluating administrators. Are the formal procedures carried out regularly and applied to all administrators? Does the institution have a way to periodically evaluate the evaluation program? Does the individual whose performance is being evaluated have access to an appeals or grievance procedure? Is confidentiality maintained? Do the procedures used employ both objective and subjective measures? Does the administrator being evaluated have full knowledge of the procedures, timetable, and results?

Also to be considered, says Nordvall (1979), is whether the administrator evaluation program has been introduced in response to faculty demand. Some faculty members believe that they should evaluate administrators just as they are evaluated by students. Nordvall warns that evaluation introduced for this reason will tend to dwell on the assessment *process* rather than on the *results.* Once the faculty members who want a hand in the evaluation of administrators have their demands satisfied, they will lose interest in whether or not administrative performance actually improves.

The literature on the evaluation of college and university administrators finds substantial support in the much larger literature on the general topic of human resource management. The theories and closely examined practices involved in human resource management apply as fully to college and university administrators as to business managers. Thus, Sashkin (1981) has identified a general set of principles to apply in judging any performance-appraisal system:

1. Are administrators rewarded for developing their subordinates?
2. Are administrators trained in the skills required of helpers and counselors?
3. Are job descriptions based on behavioral or job-relevant performance standards?
4. Are the administrators whose performance is to be assessed actively involved in the appraisal process?
5. Are performance goals set?
6. Do appraisal sessions (to review the assessment results) have a problem-solving process?
7. Is the role of judge clearly separated from the role of helper/counselor?
8. Does the appraisal system require only reasonable and essential amounts of paper work and technical administration?
9. Are peer comparisons avoided as a central feature of the appraisal process?
10. Is information needed for administrative actions accessible and effectively used?

Conclusion and Summary

The evaluation guidelines and strategies suggested in the literature are the end product of a wealth of experimentation and experience and are worth careful study. Colleges and universities considering the introduction of an administrative evaluation program or anxious to overcome remnants of resistance or ease sticking points in an existing program would do well to ponder this advice. Above all, they should proceed slowly, carefully, and candidly, as the groundwork is laid for each successive step in the evaluation program.

What are the benchmarks of successful administrative evaluation programs? The literature and experience suggest the following:

1. Involve administrators in formulating the evaluation procedures and instruments.
2. Gain genuine support from top-level administrators and be sure that this support is articulated publicly.

3. Use multiple sources of information for evaluation data.
4. Hold discussions between the administrator and his or her immediate superior, and gain agreement on the criteria and the amount of weight to be given them in the future measurement of performance.
5. Smooth the implementation of the evaluation process and avoid the common defects itemized earlier in this chapter.
6. Know that the gathering of evaluation data is not an end, only a means to an end, and ultimately involves a subjective judgment.
7. Be sure that only reliable and valid data sifted through the evaluation instruments and procedures are used.
8. Conform the appraisal program to all applicable civil rights laws and affirmative action requirements.
9. Set up an internal feedback mechanism to regularly review the evaluation program.
10. Reduce resistance to the program not by fiat or muscle but by being willing to listen to others, explain and modify the program, and allow enough time for the program's acceptance.

Also, never overlook the fundamental fact that a college or university must have a compelling reason for setting up an evaluation program in the first place. As practiced today, the predominant purpose of evaluation is to lay the foundation for subsequent decisions on contract renewal and promotion. In fact, however, the predominant purpose should be to improve administrative performance. The latter is the professed purpose at most institutions, but it is an open secret that evaluations are handy tools for personnel decisions. It is high time to turn the situation around.

This chapter has addressed the important benefits of assessing administrative performance, the principles underlying a successful evaluation program, and the pitfalls to avoid. These broad areas form the backdrop for the next chapter, which will examine several specific approaches to evaluation and spell out their advantages and disadvantages.

⊀ 3 ⊁

Evaluating
Administrative Performance:
What Works and What Doesn't

Performance appraisal has many facets. It is an exercise in observation and judgment. It is a measurement and feedback process. It is an inexact, human process that must meet key requirements if it is to succeed.

Key Requirements

An appraisal system that fails to meet the seven key requirements of relevance, sensitivity, reliability, freedom from contamination, freedom from deficiency, practicality, and acceptability is probably doomed to failure.

Relevance. There must be (1) clear links between the institution's goals and the performance standards for a particular administrative position and (2) clear links between the critical elements in the position and the elements selected for evaluation. Phrased another way, relevance can be determined by answering the question, What *really* makes the difference between success and failure in a particular position?

Sensitivity. The issue here is whether the administrative appraisal system is capable of distinguishing effective from ineffective performers. If not, effective administrators will be rated on a par with mediocre ones, and the appraisal system will be worse than useless, helpful neither for improving performance nor for making personnel decisions. Worse than useless, because an insensitive appraisal system will undermine the motivation of its participants, both the evaluators and the evaluated.

There is a significant distinction between an appraisal system designed for developmental purposes and one designed to aid in personnel decisions. Cascio (1986) comments that the appraisal system designed to promote development requires data about differences within the individual, whereas the appraisal system designed for personnel decisions requires data about differences between individuals. The two patterns of information are like two keys that open two different doors. They are definitely not interchangeable. Any attempt to design an appraisal system to meet both purposes will result in a complex and costly system. As a practical matter, reports Kavanagh (1982), what is generally gathered on campuses is information helpful in personnel decisions.

Reliability. As used here, the word refers to consistency of judgment. Appraisals of an academic dean by ten different department chairs may not coincide exactly, but they should be in general agreement. It stands to reason that raters from different vantage points (for example, the academic vice-president, deans, students) will perceive the performance of a given administrator differently. Not to admit these varying perceptions would render the judgments suspect. Each offers a unique perspective, and together, one hopes, they will paint a complete operational picture of the administrator.

In the matter of the validity or accuracy of judgments, however, Cascio (1986) observes that we do not know what "truth" really is in the appraisal of performance. But, he adds, by assuring ourselves that an appraisal system is relevant, sensitive, and reliable and by satisfying scientific and legal requirements in the structuring of the system, we can take for granted that the judgments will also be valid.

Freedom from Contamination. The performance of an administrator should be measured without the contamination of factors clearly beyond his or her control, such as economic con-

ditions, faulty or inadequate equipment, or a lack of human resource support. The purpose is to evaluate the administrator's
performance without holding him or her responsible for extra-
neous subverting influences.

Freedom from Deficiency. All relevant components of
an administrator's performance should be identified and included
in the evaluation system. Even components that are time consuming or tend to defy measurement should not be ignored or
overlooked. A failure to include one or two can easily result in a
distorted assessment.

Practicality. Appraisal instruments should be readily
understood and easily put to use by administrators, faculty, students, and others involved in the process. They should not demand an inordinate amount of time or energy to complete and
should not have to be filled out too often. A case in point was
recently encountered by the author in a small southeastern college. The evaluation system called for the academic dean to prepare monthly narrative assessments of the performances of eight
department chairs. In turn, each chair also prepared a monthly
narrative assessment of the dean. All these reports were sub-
mitted on the first of each month to the academic vice-president.
The reports made an impressive foot-high column on his desk.
At the very least, this was a case of overkill.

Acceptability. This is probably the most important re-
quirement of all. It is the foundation upon which the appraisal
edifice rests. Unless the appraisal program has won the un-
reserved support both of the evaluators and of those being evaluated, you can count on human ingenuity to find ways to subvert
and/or destroy the program. Too many colleges and universities have yet to learn this life-and-death lesson. Too many oc-
cupy themselves with the niceties of administrative evaluation
procedures and make virtually no effort to garner active support
for the program on campus. They focus their attention on the
technical soundness of the program rather than on its attitudinal and interpersonal aspects. They tend to play power games
with personnel and operate almost as a secret cabal on campus.
They would make success for the assessment program much
more likely if they would court campus personnel in frank dis-

cussions. No substitute has yet been found for the active support of administrators in the efficient operation of an assessment program.

Performance Criteria

Deciding what to evaluate is one of the most difficult problems in developing a performance evaluation system. Small wonder that evaluating an administrator's performance can be perplexing, when one considers how quickly a football fan concludes that a team's quarterback is a poor player because several of his passes have been intercepted. "An objective appraisal," says Rice (1985, p. 32), "would raise the following questions: Were the passes really bad or did the receivers run the wrong patterns? Did the offensive line give the quarterback adequate protection? Did he call those plays himself, or were they sent in by the coach? Was the quarterback recovering from an injury? . . . How good is the vision of the fan? Did he or she have a good view of the [television] set through the room's smoky haze? Was the fan talking to a friend during the game? How many beers did the fan down during the game?"

In comparison with a barroom judgment of a quarterback's performance, the evaluation of a top-level administrator is considerably more complex and consequential.

Outcomes and Behaviors. In deciding what to evaluate, it is important to consider whether the evaluation should focus on outcomes (results) or behaviors (activities). Administrators can be evaluated either on the outcomes of their departments or on their administrative behaviors.

Most administrative performance evaluations concentrate on behaviors, such as decision making, planning, organizing, and communicating. One reason for this, reports Cherrington (1987), is that administrative outcomes are hard to identify. Another reason is that outcomes can be confused and contaminated by outside factors that administrators cannot control. By comparison, the behaviors of administrators are relatively free of contaminants and more easily identified and evaluated.

However, there is an undeniable advantage to the evaluation of outcomes. The spotlight is on results, and in the minds of many, nothing equals the importance of results. Management by objectives (MBO), a results-oriented assessment, is accordingly used by some colleges and universities in the evaluation of their administrators' performance.

One potential problem arising from this orientation is that results can be, and sometimes are, accomplished by less than ethical means. Sometimes the results are obtained by illegal acts. One example should suffice: the basketball coach whose team wins twenty-five games in one season to national acclaim, while at the same time the coach is supplying illegal payoffs in the form of cars, clothes, and money to star players.

There are advantages and disadvantages, then, in orienting the evaluation system either to outcomes or to behaviors. Each can be appropriate in evaluating academic administrators. Their intended use, says Cherrington (1987), should determine which approach to select. Evaluations intended primarily for improvement of performance should focus on behaviors.

Developing Criteria. It is only fair that an appraisal of administrative performance be matched against a detailed and accurate description of the job. The clearer the job description, the more accurate the appraisal can be. Thus, the first step in evaluating performance is to scrutinize job descriptions and to develop new ones as needed. Job descriptions more than two or three years old can probably stand an update.

There is prevalent in higher education the curious presumption that administrators know what their jobs call for. This presumption is rather remote from the truth. Seldin (1983) reports that field interviews with administrators at various colleges and universities revealed that almost one-half of them were unable to nail down the specific criteria on which their performances were evaluated.

It is true that job descriptions vary widely from one administrative post to another within the same institution. It is also true that factors peculiar to the institution, having to do with traditions, goals, and priorities, will cause a job description for the same administrative position to differ in many important respects from one institution to another. Nevertheless, a review of the literature indicates that the qualities and activities usually evaluated fall into certain categories.

Sprunger and Bergquist (1978) suggest that knowledge and capacity, dependability, adaptability, interpersonal relations, commitment to professional growth, resource and personnel management, and institutional loyalty are key criteria. Skipper (1982) developed a four-variable equation to predict the administrative effectiveness of academic deans. Derived from a longer list of variables by discriminate analysis, the four variables were found to distinguish effective from ineffective deans. The four? Intellectual efficiency, flexibility, knowledge about position, and judgment.

Nordvall (1979) presents a lengthy list of criteria that are mentioned in the literature of administrative evaluation. Among others, they include:

1. *Underlying traits and interest*—adaptability, communication skills, good judgment, impartiality, initiative, integrity, intellectual and cultural interests, mental vigor, responsibility, sense of humor, trustworthiness
2. *General quality and dimensions of performance*—ability to organize, attention to details, awareness and anticipation, efficient delegation of responsibility, initiative, job knowledge, soundness of decisions, quantity of work, good judgment
3. *Interpersonal relationships*—considerate and sympathetic attitude toward faculty, other administrators, and students; effective communication with group members; cooperation; fairness; perceptive judgment of people; ability to say no effectively; willingness; ability to "open doors" for others
4. *Leadership*—inspires confidence, maintains morale of the work group, encourages participation, instills enthusiasm for institutional and personal professional goals, secures group action
5. *Professional interests*—commitment to excellence, interest in continued professional development, knowledge of new

developments and innovations in higher education, contributions to academic or administrative field, tolerance of
new ideas
6. *Commitment to institution*—concern for general welfare of
institution, participation in activities of campus community,
skill in achieving desirable public relations

Dressel (1976) addressed the question of what makes an
effective administrator by taking up the matter with former
presidents and long-term observers of academic administrators.
He suggests that effective administrators (1) develop and use
the administrative talents of subordinates; (2) support and praise
subordinates; (3) avoid favoritism, intimacies, and the obligations of covert agreements; (4) maintain distance, objectivity,
and perspective on problems and controversies unless intervention is necessary; (5) listen to and accept advice and criticism
from both supporters and antagonists, admit errors, and subsequently alter decisions and policies; (6) operate by principle
rather than by personality; (7) maintain balanced attention to
all aspects of the job; and (8) work to develop and maintain effective two-way communication.

A sampling of the criteria employed at various colleges
and universities reveals considerable differences in emphasis.
For example, in assessing departmental chairpersons, the University of Delaware focuses on leadership, success with departmental matters, decision making, and personal qualities, in addition to factors unique to a particular department. The Beaver
Campus of Pennsylvania State University concerns itself with
management style, leadership, administrative skills, and communications. Academic deans at Bucknell University (Pennsylvania) are evaluated primarily in eight areas: planning and organization, implementation, efficiency, coordination/cooperation,
collegiality, communication, creativity, and professional growth.
Bergen Community College (New Jersey) looks, among other
criteria, at planning ability, quality of leadership, initiative and
creativity, judgment, human relations, delegation of responsibility, and service to college and community.

Obstacles to Effective Appraisal of Performance

Although the obstacles to effective appraisal of performance are legion, a number of them are destructive enough to warrant special mention:

1. Up to 93 percent of appraisal programs give the immediate supervisor *sole* responsibility for the appraisal of performance, according to DeVries and others (1986).

2. Standards and ratings are mercurial and tend to fluctuate widely, and often unfairly. Some raters are tough, others are lenient. Some departments are run by very competent administrators, others seem to run themselves efficiently despite the administrators. Thus, the less competent at one institution can be awarded a higher rating than the more competent at another institution (Oberg, 1972).

3. The validity of some appraisals is questionable if those making them resist the evaluation process. Instead of bestowing negative ratings and below-average salary increases on less effective administrators, some evaluators take the easy way out by pinning an average or even above-average rating on inferior performance.

4. Appraisals at times interfere with a constructive coaching relationship between supervisor and subordinate. The appraisal interview tends to emphasize the hierarchical relationship between an academic dean and a department chair, for example, by elevating the dean to the role of judge and subordinating the teacher-learner relationship. Moreover, too many evaluators lack the interpersonal skills required for effective interviews.

5. Cousins and Rogus (1977) cite a number of evaluation concerns, including the validity of faculty judgment, derogatory publicity about the appraisal process, and misinterpreting the popularity of administrators for real worth.

6. Referring to the evaluation of academic deans, Bornholdt (1978) reports that the problems implicit in their appraisal include the difficulty of defining such a complex position and the fact that incumbent deans must often accept priorities set by predecessor deans.

7. Cherrington (1987) points to the excessive emphasis sometimes placed on numbers. An evaluator who has a numbers fetish, he says, venerates numbers, which are really the equivalent of subjective judgments, as though they were hard, objective facts.

8. Rice (1985) regrets that one-sided performance evaluations place administrators on the defensive, particularly when the evaluations turn into lectures or harangues and end with the senior administrator's commenting on "how great it's been to have this open exchange of views."

This is a daunting list of obstacles, indeed, and is calculated to give pause to any college or university contemplating the introduction of an administrative evaluation program. Yet it is no solution to decide not to institute such a program. People being what they are, off-the-cuff appraisals will always be made in organizations. It is unarguably better to install a program that requires appraisals to approach fairness and accuracy. The program turns into a reason for the esprit de corps, the loyalty, and the smooth meshing of departments. They are obstacles only before they are overcome. Then they are history.

Judgmental Data

When individuals appraise an administrator's performance, they are offering judgmental data. This is unavoidable. But these opinions or judgments of another's performance have given rise to the term *judgmental data*. It is not necessarily a term of censure, although it has become a rallying point for those who oppose evaluation programs. The disbelievers argue that evaluation programs, brimming as they are with subjective judgments, are fatally flawed and should be totally discarded. The believers, in contrast, argue that an administrator's performance cannot be added up or quantified and that human judgments about human performance necessarily are subjective. That does not mean, of course, that the judgments cannot be systematized and sanitized against bias of one kind or another. And judgments by those who have firsthand knowledge of an administrator's performance are of special value.

Judgmental data come in many forms, the most prevalent being rating scales (Llgen and Barnes-Farrell, 1984).

The Problem of Bias. Underlying the use of ratings is the presumption that the evaluator is reasonably objective and accurate. Yet few would take issue with the view that an evaluator's memory is sometimes fallible and that the evaluator may subscribe to a set of assumptions about people that may or may not be valid. The evaluator's witting or unwitting biases produce rating errors, or gaps between the "true" ratings and the ratings actually assigned. There are several common types of rating errors:

1. Halo bias, which is perhaps the most pervasive rating error, refers to the tendency of evaluators to be influenced in rating one aspect of performance by the rating they have given another. A high opinion of an administrator's performance as a leader may favorably color the administrator's rating in several other areas. A low opinion of performance in one job segment may carry over into other segments. In both cases the evaluator is somewhat blinded by an insular performance, good or bad, and then goes on to broaden that rating. Nordvall (1979) suggests that the way to mitigate this halo effect is to ask mutually exclusive questions. The evaluator is asked to place the administrator along a continuum, with "concern with getting work done is primary" and "concern with faculty satisfaction is primary" as the poles.

2. Leniency or severity bias is found when a disproportionate number of administrators receive high or low ratings. This bias is commonly attributed to a distorted view of what constitutes acceptable administrative performance. The tenderhearted give consistently high ratings while the irascible give consistently low ones. Either way, inequalities result and are manifested in salary and other personnel decisions based on the distorted evaluations. Two techniques are recommended to offset the leniency-severity bias. Persuade the rater to enroll in a training program designed to erase this bias and be sure that appraisal data come from multiple sources to minimize the impact of a given rater's bias.

Some colleges and universities approach the problem by

allocating permissible percentages in rating categories. For example, no more than 10 percent of one's subordinates can be rated outstanding; no more than 50 percent can be rated average. But many administrators and psychologists frown on the use of an arbitrary percentage, on the ground that it imprisons the evaluation process. Besides, nobody really knows in advance what the distribution curve will be. One can almost count as a by-product of the arbitrary-percentage approach a measure of resentment from evaluators and evaluated alike.

3. Central tendency bias is the predilection of some evaluators to bestow only average ratings and avoid the positive and negative ends of a rating scale. If this bias operates to the detriment of the outstanding performer, it also acts to shield the poor performer. The institution also is victimized since it is unable through its evaluation program to identify and reward top performers or help or terminate poor performers. Morale is another inevitable victim. Sashkin (1981) urges that this bias be eliminated by additional evaluation training and says that with practice evaluators can find themselves using all scale points with reasonable ease.

4. Recency bias refers to situations in which recent events have undue influence on performance appraisals. An administrator's excellent work for an entire year can be dwarfed by a single negative event just prior to his or her evaluation. Or, conversely, a year's mediocre performance can be rewarded because of a single recent success. Often, this bias simply requires detection and discussion to eliminate it. More stubborn cases, however, may require more persistent methods. Gatewood and Feild (1987) suggest keeping an activity record for the entire year so that at evaluation time this written record can be consulted for a more balanced rating. This admittedly is quite time consuming, since it entails making written notes at numerous intervals during the year, but it may be worth undertaking in the interests of fairness and accuracy. The notes should not be brief evaluations but rather nonevaluative descriptions of events and the administrator's behavior. At the very least they will exorcise the recency-bias hobgoblin.

5. Guessing bias appears when evaluators, stumped for a

meaningful judgment, offer an opinion anyway on particular aspects of an administrative performance. One can probably estimate the size of the guess by asking about the competency of the evaluator to make the judgment. The instrument can determine the frequency of meetings or communications with the administrator under evaluation, as well as the level of the rater's understanding of the administrator's duties (Phipps, 1975). Raters should be encouraged to omit responses when they feel unable to make proper judgments.

Training Raters. Certain problems of rater bias can be directly attacked by developing training methods to identify the bias and provide an approach to overcome it (Gatewood and Feild, 1987).

These training methods often rely on videotapes. In one program, as described by Latham, Wexley, and Pursell (1975), five videotaped interactions are screened. In each, an administrator is involved in rating a co-worker. At the end of each tape, the audience is asked to come up with ratings based on two questions: How would you rate this person? How do you think the administrator rated this person? Each of the five videotapes demonstrates a different kind of rating error. After the showing of each tape, there is a discussion in which the rating error is identified and analyzed, and different approaches are suggested to eliminate or minimize the error. Six months later, when the same audience was reassembled to view another set of videotapes, its performance was flawless. It had learned to detect basic rating errors.

Cascio (1986, p. 311) is persuaded that emphasis is better placed on training raters to be keener and more accurate observers of behaviors rather than on training them "how to" or "how not to" rate. This approach, he says, might contain the following steps:

1. The raters are shown a videotape of an administrator's performance on the job.
2. The raters evaluate the administrator utilizing a given rating scale.
3. Each rater's judgment is placed on a flipchart.

4. Differences in rating judgments and reasons for the differences are hotly argued in a group discussion led by the trainer.
5. The raters approach a consensus on performance standards and relative levels of effective and ineffective administrative behavior.
6. The tape is shown again.
7. The raters again evaluate the administrator, but this time supported by specific examples that are recorded by the raters.
8. The new ratings are compared to the consensus judgments of the group.
9. Individualized feedback is provided to each rater.

The key to improving the performance-appraisal process, according to Cascio (1986), is to apply certain principles of learning, which include

- encouraging raters to record examples of administrator behavior
- providing an opportunity to practice
- providing feedback and reinforcement when appropriate
- offering periodic refresher training to maintain the desired rater behaviors

Another training program uses videotapes somewhat differently. In this approach, the tapes relate basic administrative concepts to job review and career planning. The idea is to sell the importance of job-performance appraisal as a major administrative function by establishing a direct link between the appraisals and institutional strategies ("Training Managers . . . ," 1980).

Some raters consistently hand out such high ratings that they come to have no meaning. Prather (1974) reports evidence that the problem of the inflated ratings can be subdued by retraining. For example, when a branch of the federal government initiated a new appraisal program, it provided training and feedback to those who would be in a position to rate the performance of others. Part of the training consisted of observing and evaluating specimen individuals whose behavior typified the administrators to be evaluated. Ratings were discussed and analyzed and then compared to the "correct" ratings. The experience of discussing, analyzing, and comparing was a distinct aid to the raters, who were able to develop a common performance standard.

To reduce the problem of inflated ratings, some institutions use ranking procedures. Others design a new form every few years. But the problem does not lie with the form. It lies with the untrained evaluators. Thus, Cherrington (1987) urges administrators to be trained for competent evaluations. No form can replace the trained and experienced evaluator, and conversely the best form cannot compensate for the inexperience of the novice evaluator. This last point cannot be overstressed.

Evaluation Methods

Reporting on the results of their survey of approximately 400 American colleges and universities, Bergquist and Tenbrink (1977) list six major approaches to administrator evaluation: unstructured narration, unstructured documentation, structured narrative, structured documentation, rating scales, and MBO. A review of more recent literature indicates that these six are still the most prevalent approaches to administrator evaluation.

Unstructured Narration (or Essay Appraisal). In this common approach the rater describes in writing the administrator's strengths, weaknesses, and potential, together with suggestions for improving performance. The approach assumes that a candid, thoughtful statement from a rater with intimate knowledge of an administrator's performance will be as productive as any more formal and complicated method. Well done, the essay does provide a wealth of detailed information about performance. The problem is that comparisons across administrators (five deans, for example) become virtually impossible. Each essay addresses different aspects of each administrator's performance. Thus, the essay approach clearly does not lend itself to personnel decisions. Methods comparing the performance of different administrators are more suitable for this purpose.

Unstructured Documentation. In this approach the administrator is asked to document activities and successes in letters of recommendation, daily logs, interview data, and ratings of participants in programs operated by the administrator. The approach primarily involves self-directed evaluation and falls short of constituting a formal program. Nor does it produce data on activities and successes or on objectives and failures during the evaluation period. Sprunger and Bergquist (1978) report that most unstructured documentation is based on implicit, not explicit, criteria. And when the criteria are explicit, the selection precludes an objective assessment since the administrator selects the documentation for his or her evaluation. No administrator is likely to admit his or her faults.

Structured Narration. This approach requires the evaluator to respond to a series of short-answer questions about the administrator's performance. Typical are the questions asked by a southwestern community college:

- In what area does this administrator demonstrate the greatest strength?
- In what area does this administrator demonstrate the greatest need for improvement?
- If you overheard your colleagues discussing the performance of this administrator, what would they likely be saying?
- Discuss the initiative and creativity of this administrator.
- Describe two instances in which you have seen the vitality of this administrator.
- To what extent has this administrator accomplished the following objective? . . .

Structured Documentation. Structured documentation has been used for years in the creative and performing arts, but only recently has it been adapted to administrative evaluation in higher education. This approach calls on the supervisor and the administrator to agree on the performance categories appropriate to the administrator's work. On occasion, subordinates, peers, instructional staff, and others are asked to participate in this selection process. Those in a good position to affirm or deny the administrator's proclaimed successes are usually chosen. Typically, the categories relate to job functions, skill areas, or performance objectives. The burden of documenting each claimed success falls to the administrator. A drawback to this approach is that it provides only noncompetitive evidence unrelated to any standard. But the approach has use in that it can assist in role clarification and team building and can be fitted in effectively in an array of developmental programs.

Rating Scales. This is certainly the most widely prevalent method of appraising administrative performance. Locher and Teel (1977) state that rating scales are used more than all other evaluation methods combined. Many types of scales are used in this method. Table 1 presents some of the more popularly used scales. Scale A assigns numbers to scale points and has the words *low* and *high* at each end of the scale. Scale B is an adjectival continuum from *unsatisfactory* to *exceptional*. Scale C is deemed superior (Gatewood and Feild, 1987) because scale

Table 1. Examples of Rating Scales.

Job Dimension: Completion of Long-Range Planning Reports

Thoroughness of data sources used, completeness of statistical analysis, and clarity of recommendations.

(A)	1 Low	2	3	4	5 High
(B)	Unsatisfactory	Below Average	Average	Good	Exceptional
	___	___	___	___	___
(C)	1 Reports are not satisfactory	2 Reports contain a number of errors	3 Reports are generally acceptable with few errors	4 Reports are thorough and complete	5 Reports are well analyzed and carefully reasoned

Source: Adapted from Gatewood and Feild, 1987.

points are described in terms of the adequacy of performance in preparing reports. Other aspects of performance are equally pragmatic and specific.

Discrete scales, such as those in Table 1, generally have a spread of at least three categories and sometimes more than twenty categories. Although experienced evaluators can handle up to ten categories without problem, rating consistency drops sharply when there are fewer than four or more than ten categories (Rice, 1985). Actually, five to nine categories seem to produce the most consistent ratings.

Rating instruments generally exclude any normative references against which performance can be measured. However, Fisher (1977) suggests six such references: the performance of predecessors in the position, other individuals in similar positions, an "ideal" performance, one's past performance, one's performance goals, and the performance expectation of others. In contrast, Dressel (1976, p. 395) argues that norms are "virtually meaningless" since each administrator is unique and each administrator's effectiveness depends on personal traits and capabilities as well as on the institution's characteristics.

As a method of evaluation, rating scales do have some weaknesses. For example, they are usually not tailored to the specific position being evaluated. Students, faculty, trustees, and other administrators may hold contrary views on what constitutes high performance. Actually, the professional values of the administrator and the raters may be polar opposites. The characteristics singled out for appraisal may be inappropriate or incorrectly scaled or improperly combined into a total. Nor do rating scales tend to yield the depth of understanding found in thoughtful narrative appraisals.

Despite these weaknesses, rating scales are enormously popular, and for good reason. They are far less time consuming to develop and administer than other evaluation methods—no small consideration when dealing with overburdened personnel. The results can be expressed in quantitative terms, a psychological reassurance that the method is an objective one. Any number and kind of performance dimensions can be considered. Lastly, the rating scales permit a ready and, on the face, unchallengeable comparison among administrators.

Interestingly, rating scales, though frequently criticized, have proved just as reliable and valid (King, Hunter, and Schmidt, 1980) as the more sophisticated approaches to performance evaluation. And they are much more acceptable to raters than other methods (Berkshire and Highland, 1953).

In the use of any rating forms, say Surwill and Heywood (1976), certain operating principles should be followed: (1) the activities rated should be in the job description; (2) the rater should be in a position to observe the behavior rated and make a valid judgment about it; (3) the person being evaluated should take part in the design, administration, and review of the form; and (4) raters should have the option of not responding when they are unable to make a judgment.

Additional guidelines, offered by Llgen and Barnes-Farrell (1984), recommend that performance dimensions should be (1) behavior oriented ("gets report in on time") rather than trait oriented ("is reliable") and (2) defined in such straightforward, specific terms that all raters will share a common interpretation. It is also preferable, they say, for the choices of ratings ("anchors"), which define the different response categories on each scale, to be tied whenever possible to specific behavioral examples.

Management by Objectives (MBO). Traditionally, the personal traits of administrators have often been used as criteria for evaluating performance. In this case the evaluating supervisor plays the role of judge. In MBO, however, the situation is reversed. The focus of the appraisal process shifts from the administrator's personal attributes to job performance. The evaluating supervisor sheds judicial robes and becomes a counselor and facilitator (Mondy and Noe, 1984). MBO is a result-oriented rating method that relies on goal setting to establish objectives for the entire college or university, for each administrative unit, and for each administrator.

How are these objectives established? The administrator and the administrator's supervisor meet for three purposes: (1) to agree on the administrator's major objectives in an allotted time period (perhaps a year); (2) to develop plans detailing how and when the objectives are to be achieved; and (3) to agree on the yardsticks that will determine if the objectives have been met.

Reviews are held periodically to measure progress toward the objectives. At the end of the allotted time, the administrator and supervisor evaluate the results and develop objectives for the next period.

Among the institutions that operate or have adapted MBO programs are Austin College (Texas), New College of the University of Alabama, Delgado Community College (Louisiana), Gordon College (Massachusetts), Fairleigh Dickenson University (New Jersey), Furman University (South Carolina), University of the Redlands (California), and the University of Tennessee, Martin.

Lahti (1978) comments that the most significant objectives for goal setting are to provide feedback to each person, to furnish superiors with data on which to make personnel decisions, to serve as a basis for observing behavior so as to improve performance, and to encourage staff development.

Like all approaches to appraisal, MBO has a number of advantages and disadvantages, some patent, others more subtle. Lahti (1978) spells out the following advantages: Administrators know in advance how they will be evaluated. The administrator and supervisor agree on the content and expectations of the administrator's job. The process has a self-correcting, personal-growth characteristic that helps people set challenging and attainable goals. The process helps uncover individual development needs, and the actual record of performance is scrutinized instead of the administrator's personality traits.

Allen (1986) adds another advantage: MBO ties together the needs of individuals, administrative units, and the institution. Finally, Seldin (1980a) finds that minimizing the penalty for failure and maximizing the potential for reward encourage a spirit of administrative innovation and experimentation.

At bottom, of course, MBO appraisals are just as open to claims of unfairness as are other systems of performance evaluation. Trying to set reasonable goals well in advance is no mean task. Many goals are vulnerable to the economic, social, and political conditions in society at the time, and a single administrator can do little about these conditions. Beyond that, the method's very individuality makes it difficult, if not impossible, to compare the performance of one administrator with that of another (Bernardin and Beatty, 1984). And isn't that a key purpose of performance review?

Kondrasuk (1981) points out that an effective MBO system often takes three to five years to implement. Few colleges and universities can, or are willing to, make that kind of commitment. It comes as no surprise, then, that MBO systems often fall by the wayside.

Also, MBO appraisals require sizable amounts of time and paper work (Winstead, 1979); they do not provide diagnostic information to determine why an individual is not performing (Cascio, 1986); and administrators often lack the high-level writing and coaching skills needed to implement such a sophisticated management practice (Sprunger and Bergquist, 1978).

Mixed Systems of Administrative Evaluation. The six approaches discussed above are not infrequently combined or expanded in an institutional evaluation system. Hoyle (1973) suggests, as a useful first step to establishing a long-range evaluation system, that an institution employ a survey instrument that rates the perceptions of a dean by his or her constituents. Fisher and Howell (1972) advise that evaluation forms should be filled out at random by visitors to administrative offices to determine if the visitors were well served. Ehrle (1975) describes an instrument for the evaluation of department chairs that includes uniform procedures; a written set of performance criteria; and input from faculty on the subjects of problem solving, relations with students and colleagues, decision making, communication, operations, and delegation of responsibility.

Sprunger and Bergquist (1978) suggest comparing the actual rating results with the anticipated ratings by the administrator. Rice (1985) sees behaviorally anchored rating scales (BARS) as offering promise. The anchors—that is, the opposite ends of the scale—define the ratings on a scale. For example, for "perseverance" a BARS scale might offer choices ranging from "keeps working on difficult task until job is completed" to "likely to stop work on a hard job at the first sign of difficulty." Morris (1981) believes that, in the end, a dean's evaluation turns out to be a faculty self-portrait. If faculty members feel good about themselves and their colleagues, he says, the chances are favorable that both college and dean are doing well.

Conclusion

Despite much progress in administrative evaluation, the bad news is that there is no simple way to assess performance. Certainly, the notion of a precise method of appraisal is appealing, but it is highly unlikely that a way will ever be found to measure the entirety of complex behavior with one yardstick. The kernel of good news, however, is that much of the concern over rating scales and evaluation formats seems to have been unwarranted. If anything has been learned, it is that there is no single "correct" way to evaluate administrative performance. There are many ways. Given certain statistical corrections, the correlations between scores on alternative rating formats are very high. All the formats measure essentially the same thing (Cascio, 1986). Colleges and universities should feel free to experiment to find the method that feels "right" to them.

The next chapter will focus on planning, implementing, and managing a successful evaluation system. It will discuss among other topics what should be evaluated, who should carry out the evaluation, and when it should be done.

⊀ 4 ⊁

Planning, Implementing, and Managing a Successful Evaluation Program

In developing an administrative evaluation program, a crucial question is, who should evaluate the performance? It is often erroneously presumed that the administrator's immediate supervisor is in the best and most appropriate position to do the evaluation. But in truth this often is not so.

Who actually is in the best position to produce objective and meaningful evaluations of academic administrators? Clearly, the answer varies from institution to institution. However, in general there are six levels of individuals or groups potentially capable of assessing administrative performance: the administrator's immediate supervisor, peers in the institution, faculty members, subordinates, clients served, and the administrator himself or herself.

In any college or university the administrative positions are legion and diverse. In the interest of clarity and brevity, this book confines itself to evaluation of the president, academic vice-president or provost, deans, and department chairs. It should be evident, however, that the same factors involved in planning, implementing, and managing a successful evaluation program for these key administrators are also applicable to all other administrative positions.

An Overview

Before weighing the advantages and disadvantages of different evaluators, let us briefly consider several general issues. Experience teaches us that some evaluators are able to perceive certain behaviors more clearly and objectively than other behaviors. Subordinates, for example, may be the best judges of how fair and understanding an administrator is in dealing with others. Supervisors may be the best judges of a subordinate's ability to meet deadlines. Llgen and Barnes-Farrell (1984) conclude, therefore, that a crucial characteristic of different raters is the effect of their viewpoint on their ability to appraise the administrator's behaviors.

A collateral issue centers on the motivation of the rater. Raters may be biased positively or negatively. It is well established that self-evaluations tend to be more positive than ratings by supervisors. Similarly, when supervisors sit down with subordinates to discuss ratings in detail, they tend to give higher ratings to avoid some of the interpersonal tension inherent in discussing poor performance (Fisher, 1979).

Supervisors. The supervisor is generally the evaluator of the subordinate's performance. In the academic hierarchy, presidents evaluate vice-presidents, who in turn evaluate deans, who in turn evaluate department chairs. Why? Because of the belief that the immediate supervisor is the person most familiar with the subordinate's performance. And who can argue against the value of firsthand observations? The fact of the matter is, however, that supervisors at times produce inaccurate ratings. They do not always observe firsthand what the subordinates actually do. And even when they do, they may lack the expertise necessary for proper appraisal. An academic dean, for example, may supervise an admissions director. A vice-president may supervise the director of the computer information system. It would be difficult, to say the least, for the supervisor to judge performance in such cases.

Despite these problems and complexities, supervisor ratings are, and probably will continue to be, the mainstay of performance evaluation systems. But this should not be considered a fatal flaw. Many supervisors are truly excellent sources, gatherers, and interpreters of evaluative data. Prudence, however, recommends that the evaluation process be broadened to include appropriate additional raters so that the performance judgment rests on a wide base.

Peers. Peers are in a position to provide a special perspective on performance beyond the supervisor's field of vision. Nordvall (1979) urges the seeking out of peer opinion since peers interact frequently with the administrator under evaluation. Llgen and Barnes-Farrell (1984) concur and state that peer ratings frequently turn out to be more valid than supervisory evaluations. They suggest two explanations for this. First, peers perform similar jobs so they have a more intimate understanding of what should be done and how it should be done. Second, they generally cross paths with the administrator being evaluated more frequently than does the supervisor.

Cherrington (1987) adds a warning note. He says three conditions must be met before using peer appraisals: There must be (1) a high level of interpersonal trust, (2) a noncompetitive reward system, and (3) opportunities for peers to observe each other's performances. If any one of these conditions is absent, the intrinsic value of peer ratings suffers a sharp drop.

Peer appraisals do help paint a more accurate and complete portrait of an administrator's performance. But it should never be overlooked that peer appraisals need supplementing from whatever sources offer additional data or a special perspective on the administrator being evaluated (Cascio, 1986).

Faculty. If it is true that professors can be helped by student ratings, it is equally true that administrators can be helped to improve their performance by faculty ratings (Hillway, 1973; Miller, 1985). Some directors and central administrators, such as the registrar and director of financial aid, work in relative isolation and would probably not benefit from faculty ratings. But college and university presidents, academic vice-presidents, deans, and department chairs regularly interact with faculty members and should be evaluated by them. Farmer (1978) points out that, in addition to these four classes of administrators, some directors of service departments, such as the director of computer services and the director of sponsored grants and projects, are also candidates for faculty rating because of their extensive interaction with faculty members.

In fact, according to Farmer, administrators at times request faculty members with whom they work to evaluate their performance. This practice can produce valuable feedback to the administrator. But one caution is in order. To require signed evaluations practically guarantees a sharp reduction in voluntary faculty participation. And even the evaluations that are made will tend to be too general and too laudatory. Unsigned evaluations are thus preferable to signed ones.

Nevertheless, the concept of faculty evaluation of administrators has met with opposition. It has been argued that a negative faculty appraisal would have a harmful effect on the future performance of the administrator. It has also been argued that it is unrealistic to expect to recruit administrators and direct them to make changes with negative faculty impact without inviting faculty retribution at evaluation time. But these arguments have been found wanting both on theoretical grounds and in actual practice (Cousins and Rogus, 1977; Seldin, 1983; Miller, 1985).

On balance, there are compelling reasons why faculty members should participate in the appraisal of academic administrators. They have a unique perspective. Their opinions deserve a hearing and should be solicited. Their voices should be added to those of the administrator's supervisor, peers, and his or her own voice in self-evaluation, among others, in a collective judgment of the administrator's performance.

Subordinates. Although evaluations of supervisors by subordinates might seem at first blush to constitute a reversal of natural roles, they can prove quite useful when accomplished properly. Subordinates are informed, rightly or wrongly, but usually rightly, about supervisory competency from a distinct vantage point. Deans know firsthand how well the academic vice-president plans and organizes, communicates, and offers leadership. Department chairs know firsthand whether the academic dean exercises good judgment, anticipates and heads off future problems, and deals effectively with people.

Dressel (1976) points out that subordinates often worry that their criticism, no matter how well intentioned, can bring retaliation if their anonymity is not maintained. In addition to fear of reprisal, there are other problems inherent in subordinate appraisals. There is an underlying resentment in some supervisors at being evaluated by subordinates. Some subordinates will parrot only what they think their supervisors want to hear, while others will resist rating their supervisors because they think it is "improper" for subordinates to do so.

Given the nature of the supervisor-subordinate relationship in most colleges and universities, it is evident that ratings by subordinates are more valuable for improving performance than for making personnel decisions. Subordinates can provide sharp profiles of administrative effectiveness. Dyer (1974) says that their comments are specially useful when these comments are at odds with an administrator's self-evaluation. When subordinates generally disagree with an administrator's self-evaluation, that alone can provide enough motivation for the administrator to reexamine his or her performance with an eye toward changing it. As a dean at a western college commented: "The eight department chairs here rarely agree on anything. When they told me, as a group, that my leadership style was abrasive and my communications a bit confusing, I disagreed with them. But I began to think about it."

Subordinate evaluation can put an additional piece of the appraisal puzzle in place. But it takes considerable trust and candor between supervisor and subordinate and considerable maturity on the part of both to make it work.

Clients Served. In general, anyone who is in a position to observe the behaviors of an administrator should be included in the evaluation process (Cherrington, 1987). That means there are occasions when clients should be asked for their views. In evaluating a vice-president for institutional development, for example, it would be appropriate to survey a sample of individuals from whom contributions were solicited. In assessing a dean of students, it would be appropriate to sample students for views on the scope of student activities or the quality of student residence facilities.

Although the client's objectives cannot be expected to coincide with those of the college or university, Cascio (1986) is persuaded that the client's input is worthwhile in personnel decisions and the improvement of performance.

Self-Appraisal. Academic administrators always seem to be engaged in the process of self-evaluation, usually in an informal and casual way but also at times in a more organized and systematic manner. Self-evaluation has its proponents as well as its detractors. Meyer (1980) points out that self-evaluation as a component of a broader appraisal, especially if goal setting is an objective, can reinforce motivation and reduce defensiveness during the appraisal interview. Cherrington (1987) believes that self-appraisal frequently is the precursor of improved performance because it increases commitment to institutional goals.

On the negative side, self-appraisals tend to be too laudatory and to depart too much from the judgment of others (Thornton, 1980). Since it is known that administrators tend to rate themselves more highly than do their supervisors, their self-appraisals have to be approached with caution. They are not particularly useful for personnel decisions, but they have unquestionable value for personnel development and identification of training needs. To ask an administrator for a self-appraisal when he or she is being considered for promotion or a pay increase is like asking a faculty member for a self-appraisal when he or she is up for tenure. Why would any academic facing a major personnel decision willingly provide a list of professional shortcomings?

But a self-appraisal used in conjunction with, say, a supervisor's appraisal can yield useful information. If the administrator's evaluation form is identical to the one completed by the supervisor, it presents the opportunity for the two of them to discuss the similarities and differences in their views.

In summary, there are six sources of information used to evaluate administrative performance. These sources and their special uses are shown in Table 2.

Combining Sources of Data. Returning to the question of who should evaluate, we must keep in mind that the six approaches cited are not mutually exclusive. Many are used in combination. In the periodic evaluation of its dean, for example,

Table 2. Sources and Uses of Administrative Appraisal Data.

	Use	
Source	Personnel Decisions	Performance Improvement
Supervisor	X	X
Peers	X	X
Faculty	X	X
Subordinates		X
Clients served	X	X
Self-appraisal		X

the University of Delaware solicits data from department chairs, university administrators, a sampling of faculty members, staff, and students. A northeastern college evaluates its academic vice-president by collecting data from faculty, staff, alumni, department chairs, peers, and a student sample. The board of regents at Southeast Missouri State University evaluates the president on the basis of data obtained from university employees, alumni, students, area legislators, and community leaders.

Frequency of Evaluation. For high-ranking administrators, such as presidents, chancellors, academic vice-presidents, and deans, formal evaluations are generally scheduled every three to five years. Nordvall (1979) suggests that this protracted time frame probably results from the complex methods used to evaluate these administrators. Lower-ranking administrators are generally evaluated less comprehensively but more frequently, perhaps yearly. To avoid the bunching of evaluations at one time, they frequently are scheduled on the anniversary of employment.

When performance is evaluated as infrequently as every five years, raters must plumb their memories and consult their diaries to recall what the administrator did over the previous sixty months—a truly formidable task. Bernardin and Beatty (1984) report that biased ratings may be the result. Who can reconstruct in detail and accurately what was observed four or five years ago? Without the aid of a diary to refresh their minds, raters really cannot be expected to recall the specifics of effective and ineffective administrative episodes. Raters should be encouraged, therefore, to jot down brief reports of relevant events as they occur. These reports, called *critical incidents*, focus on behaviors rather than on traits. For example: "Completed the Rhinebeck project on time and within budget despite two key associates being ill."

Another approach to the appraisal-every-five-years problem is to do interim small-scale appraisals tied to the completion of major tasks or the passing of milestones on important projects. This has the additional advantage of sending a number of clear messages to the administrator. The objective is to avoid "surprises," and a good way to do this is to provide more frequent feedback to the administrator.

There may be no more important reason for formal evaluation of an academic administrator than to obtain factual information that can be used to decide whether or not to renew his term of office. A number of colleges and universities provide for annual evaluation of academic administrators, but the more common practice is to conduct a comprehensive performance review prior to the end of the term of office or after a specified number of years. Some institutions offer an "early" review upon request. For example, the University of Wisconsin at Stevens Point evaluates department chairs, associate deans, and certain other administrators in the last year of their term or every five years depending on the position. But evaluations can be triggered by presentation of a petition to the dean signed by at least one-third of the faculty and academic staff in the unit.

At the University of Delaware, the dean undergoes an in-depth review and evaluation that may be initiated by the president or provost, by petition of a simple majority of the college faculty, or even by the dean himself or herself. At Southeast Missouri State University, the president is normally evaluated every four years, but an extraordinary review may be initiated at any time by the board of regents or the faculty senate.

Implementing Performance Appraisal Systems

How an evaluation is put into place is just as critical as *what* system is used. Consider the brash approach used by a president of a midwestern university: "Convinced that an administrative assessment program was needed, the president sent a detailed form and the following memorandum to all academic administrators: 'It is the policy of this university to evaluate the performance of all administrators each year. Effective immediately, all administrators will use the enclosed form for that purpose. I look forward to the success of the program.' "

The ground swell of protest was so strong and voluble that the surprised president withdrew the memorandum within a few months. It happens much too often, however, that administrative evaluation programs are introduced into colleges and universities by presidential fiat, even though this virtually foredooms the program.

To implement a performance appraisal system requires a series of carefully planned steps. And just as two individuals do not cross a brook in the same way, no two institutions will implement an evaluation system in the same way. However, as DeVries and others (1986) point out, there are certain steps that are crucial to success in the implementation of all appraisal systems.

Examine the Givens. Before initiating a redesign effort to improve the existing performance appraisal system, consider the following questions:

- Why are we really thinking about redesigning the system?
- What organizational commitment is behind a redesign effort?
- What can we realistically expect to accomplish within a specified time frame?
- Do we have sufficient resources, financial and human, to carry out the effort?
- How and why is it important to redesign the evaluation system now in place?

Select a Development Group. Not only must those selected as members of the development group be knowledgeable and favorably oriented to the task, but they must also have credibility with the institutional staff. In addition, they must have ready access to the senior administrators who will eventually accept or reject the evaluation program. The group should be kept small, about five to eight individuals, and should include experienced academic administrators and human resource department specialists.

Some colleges and universities bring in an outside consultant—a specialist in performance appraisal systems—to join the development group. This is desirable if the necessary expertise for designing a psychometrically sound appraisal system is lacking on campus. As the academic vice-president of a California college explained, "This is a small liberal arts college, and we just don't have the expertise to develop a good system by ourselves. So we called in a consultant for six days over a couple of months. It was expensive but worth it."

Review Appraisal and Related Practices. McCall (1978a) suggests that prior to redesigning an evaluation system, the development group should review the institution's appraisal policies and practices. The group should also look into other feedback systems, legal issues, institutional philosophy, and organizational climate. Questionnaires and interviews are sometimes used to determine administrative opinions on the strengths and weaknesses of the appraisal system and to elicit recommendations for improvement.

Evaluate the Organizational Context. Evaluation systems do not operate in a vacuum. They interact with every part of the college or university. Thus, DeVries and others (1986) urge that the performance appraisal system be (1) consistent with the institution's philosophy and practice, (2) consistent with the nature of administrative work patterns, (3) in compliance with legal requirements, (4) administered at a high level in the institution (such as the office of the academic vice-president), (5) positively linked with organizational rewards for compensation and promotion, and (6) accorded active and public support by top-level academic administrators.

Develop a Complete Program. Only after examining givens and evaluating contextual factors should the development group turn its attention to the process of designing a program. DeVries and others (1986) state that the process typically involves the following tasks:

- Drafting organizational performance appraisal policy
- Conducting job analyses

- Developing appropriate forms and worksheets
- Establishing monitoring procedures
- Making necessary links with other human resource programs at policy and procedural levels
- Assessing information and skills needed for training (development)
- Testing out the measurement/feedback/training needs/monitoring loop to see if it fits together

Installation: Some Stepping-Stones. After the administrative evaluation program has been designed or redesigned, it needs to be introduced into the college or university. The best way to do this is to set forth, accurately and completely, the rationale behind the program. This includes an explanation of the policies and procedures to be used, an explanation of the terminology on the appraisal forms, and a step-by-step explanation of the development of the evaluation system.

Individuals may know what they are supposed to do and why they are supposed to do it, but that is no assurance that they actually can perform their allotted tasks. DeVries and others (1986) report two sets of skills as requisites—rating skills and feedback or communication skills. They can be developed by training supervisors in evaluation and feedback techniques (Spool, 1978; Ivancevich, 1979). Training supervisors to conduct formal appraisals and provide worthwhile feedback to administrators can be invaluable in introducing a program.

In addition, the appraisal program can be phased into a college or university by pilot testing the program on a small number of administrators. If the procedures and forms are field tested in advance, the problem areas can be identified and corrected before the program is implemented.

A university in Texas, for example, selected its college of business administration for the initial introduction and testing of a revised appraisal program. A New Jersey community college approached a revised evaluation program from a different direction. The program was phased into the institution by commencing with the top-ranking administrator—the president—and then working down the administrative ladder. By serving as a role model, the president encouraged subordinates to participate more willingly in the appraisal program.

DeVries and others (1986) recommend that after an appraisal program is implemented it should be reevaluated and any problems corrected. Program corrections will suggest themselves by the answers to certain questions: First, was the system introduced and installed as designed? Second, are administrators and their supervisors using the system as intended? Third, are the planned purposes and results of the system being attained? Fourth, does the system fit into the organizational context of the college or university? DeVries and others state that the evaluation process does not have to meet the requirements of formal research to be considered functional. Incorporating information gathering into existing organizational systems will allow an institution to gauge the success of the performance appraisal system.

Appraisal Procedures and Forms. Appraisal forms are quite helpful in systematizing the variables used in evaluating performance. A number of different models are available and can be adapted—not simply adopted—by colleges and universities seeking to design or revise a performance appraisal system. Iona College (New York) has developed a comprehensive process for evaluating academic deans for purposes of contract renewal. The college's executive vice-president and vice-president for academic affairs described it this way (Richard DeMaria, private correspondence, April 1987):

> Every two years the academic deans are evaluated for purposes of contract renewal. The following process has been employed in the last six evaluations. The vice-president writes to the following persons requesting their observations in writing on the administrative capacities and incapacities of the dean:
>
> 1. The chairs of all departments in the dean's school. They are asked to reflect the thinking of the department's members in their comments.

2. Two faculty members from the dean's school who serve on the Committee on Rank, Tenure, and Awards and two faculty members from the Committee on Curricular and Departmental Affairs.
3. The administrators in the Office of the Dean.
4. Several administrators from other offices who interact regularly with the dean (for example, the registrar or dean of admissions).
5. Student members of the academic senate.

All respondents are asked for an overall recommendation with regard to contract renewal. They are invited to meet privately with the vice-president if they wish to explain their written views in greater detail.

The vice-president also makes a public announcement in a campus newspaper to the effect that the evaluation is being conducted, and invites any faculty member to write individually instead of being represented by the department chair.

The vice-president then develops a summary statement of the evaluations, including a tabulation of the recommendations for and against reappointment; presents the data to the Executive Council; makes the council privy to the recommendation to be made to the president; asks the council members for their advice.

The vice-president discusses the summary statement with the dean and, when renewal is recommended, utilizes the statement as a starting point for setting a future agenda.

Indiana University, Bloomington, has a formal procedure that allows the faculty to have a say in the assessment of academic deans. The purpose is to provide a structured mechanism for feedback and advice for the improvement of campus administration and for the maintenance of superior administrative performance. The university's Review Committee is given a job de-

scription of the administrator under review. Evaluation procedures are at the discretion of the Review Committee provided
the committee comes up with data that at the very least answer
the following questions:

- Has the administrator set valid objectives for the unit?
- To what extent does the administrator facilitate the achievement of these objectives?
- How effectively does the administrator represent and promote the unit to outside persons?
- How well does the administrator defend the unit against outside pressures?
- How is the unit perceived on campus and by the state and
  nation?
- How effectively has the administrator implemented the university's affirmative action plan?

A liberal arts college in Texas assesses the performance of
the academic vice-president on the basis of feedback from faculty and staff members. A twelve-page rating form has multiple-
choice questions and space for comments. Raters are asked to
indicate how effectively the vice-president

- facilitates faculty research and scholarship
- facilitates faculty service
- enhances the quality of instruction
- provides leadership in planning, funding, and assessment of
  programs
- contributes to the college's reputation
- consults with deans, faculty, and faculty committees
- makes himself or herself accessible to members of the college community
- maintains impartiality in resolving conflicts
- nurtures a favorable atmosphere for collegiality
- provides leadership in institutional planning
- promotes professional development of deans and faculty
- makes decisions in planning for and implementing reductions
  in force

- represents the college outside the institution
- promotes the institution's commitment to affirmative action

Bucknell University has developed a general rating scale to be tailored to specific administrative positions. The form (see Exhibit 1 in the Appendix to this chapter) may be supplemented by sources of information and documentation, awards, participation in professional workshops and seminars, and publications and reports. A brief self-evaluation summarizing performance is often requested to provide additional light on the administrator's objectives. The results of the evaluation are discussed by the supervisor with the administrator, who initials the form to indicate that it has been discussed. The administrator may file an explanatory comment or dissent as an appendix to the evaluation.

A New Jersey community college uses an evaluation report designed to inventory strengths and weaknesses and to outline, if warranted, a practical improvement program. The report focuses on eleven components of administrative performance, with the components drawn from the job description. The raters indicate the degree of administrative effectiveness for each component (see Exhibit 2 in the Appendix to this chapter).

The College of Humanities and Sciences at Virginia Commonwealth University has developed a singular approach to evaluating the academic dean. Faculty members complete an evaluation form by indicating their perception of the relative importance of thirty-eight characteristics and rating the dean's performance on each characteristic (see Exhibit 3 in the Appendix to this chapter). As part of the evaluation, department chairs are interviewed for approximately one hour for their judgments of the dean's effectiveness. Although the interview is largely open-ended, it centers on topics such as leadership, managerial ability, accessibility, fairness in allocating resources, and ability to balance college policies and department autonomy.

Tucker and Bryan (1987) suggest that the process of differential diagnosis may be a useful model for the academic dean to follow when assessing a department chair against whom complaints have been lodged. The process is based on a review of a composite list of possible shortcomings that may be causing the chair's difficulties (see Exhibit 4 in the Appendix to this chapter). The review's objective is to rule out as many shortcomings as possible so as to concentrate on those remaining. If sufficiently serious, they can be treated by counseling or other remedial action. The authors report that the differential diagnosis model is useful in reviewing the management behavior of department chairs annually, even if no shortcomings are apparent.

A Wisconsin institution has developed a general purpose questionnaire for evaluating academic administrators. The rating form is in two parts, an evaluation section (see Exhibit 5 in the Appendix to this chapter) and an identification section. In the latter section, respondents are asked to indicate their primary appointment and length of service to the institution. They are also asked to indicate how knowledgeable they are about the administrator whom they are evaluating by checking one of the following: (1) I have regular and frequent contact with this administrator, understand the position very well, and I am familiar with this administrator's performance; (2) I have regular contact with this administrator, and I am aware of the job performance; (3) I have occasional contact, and I have some knowledge of this administrator's job performance; (4) I know this administrator, but I am not knowledgeable about the position; (5) I know who this administrator is, but not personally and my evaluation is based on my contacts with this administrator's office; (6) I have little or no contact with this administrator and/or office and, therefore, feel unqualified to offer an evaluation.

At Southeast Missouri State University, the deans, department chairs, and faculty members take part in the review of the provost. All participants are given a detailed statement describing the role, responsibilities, review, and selection of the provost. They are advised to read the statement carefully before evaluating the provost's performance. The form is notable since it asks raters to indicate (1) the extent of their contact with the provost, (2) their university service role, and (3) the five to seven functions they regard as most important and least important to the provost's role (see Exhibit 6 in the Appendix to this chapter).

San Francisco State University has produced a form for administrative evaluation, requiring of raters a narrative response (as opposed to a checkoff). Respondents are asked to complete the questionnaire (see Exhibit 7 in the Appendix to this chapter) by describing their perceptions of the administrator's effectiveness in leadership, management, decision making, communication, and professional development. This appraisal form is still in the development stage.

The Center for Faculty Evaluation and Development at Kansas State University has constructed a chairperson evaluation system that is available to colleges and universities on a fee-for-service basis. The Decad System identifies any discrepancies between the chairperson's ratings and the department colleagues' ratings on the importance of certain activities to the department or division (see Exhibit 8 in the Appendix to this chapter). The system identifies strengths and weaknesses to help the chairperson improve administrative effectiveness.

The Beaver Campus of the Pennsylvania State University offers a two-year degree program to a student body of approximately 1,200. Most students then transfer to complete their bachelor's degree. The director of academic affairs has put together a general purpose questionnaire (see Exhibit 9 in the Appendix to this chapter) to enable faculty members and staff to review the performance of administrators objectively.

Although most evaluation forms are several pages in length, a shorter version, running just one page, has been developed by a liberal arts college in Minnesota. Designed for feedback from faculty members on the performance of the academic dean, the form (see Exhibit 10 in the Appendix to this chapter) includes questions requiring both narrative responses and responses geared to a rating scale.

A different approach has been worked out by the University of Tennessee, Martin. This institution, in evaluating faculty performance, relies in part on MBO. Its planning and assessment form (see Exhibit 11 in the Appendix to this chapter) contains statements of objectives, methods of assessment, and required support. The form, prepared for evaluating faculty performance, can readily be adapted for evaluating administrative performance.

At the University of Illinois, Urbana-Champaign, college deans and committees responsible for evaluating deans, directors, heads, and chairpersons can consult a seven-page report for suggestions and guidelines in the planning and conducting of performance evaluations. Prepared by the coordinator of administrator evaluation, the report raises the following key questions to be considered when contemplating administrative evaluation:

1. What are the institution's policies on administrator evaluation?
2. What are the responsibilities of an evaluation committee? (Develop an evaluation plan? Select or design instruments? Interpret the information collected? Discuss the results of evaluation with anyone?)
3. What areas of performance should be included in the evaluation? (Performance of assigned and expected tasks? Administrative style?)
4. From whom should evaluative information be obtained? (Faculty? Academic professionals and nonacademic staff? Administrator being evaluated? Colleagues from other units? External advisory committees? Records?)
5. What method(s) should be used to collect the evaluative information? (Written survey or questionnaire? Open-ended questions? Interviews? Open meetings?)
6. How should evaluative information be summarized and interpreted?
7. What information should be distributed to whom and how?

The Appraisal Interview. This can be an uncomfortable experience for both administrators and their supervisors. Some supervisors deal with this discomfort by postponing the interview indefinitely. But that only puts off what inevitably must be faced. Worse, it also delays the corrective actions necessary to improve administrative performance. The interview must be handled well; otherwise it may leave a residue of anger, disappointment, and resentment. Instead of enhancing future administrative performance, the mishandled interview is likely to lessen initiative and produce a sense of despair and defeat, according to Wooten (1981) and Mondy and Noe (1984).

Some useful advice distilled from experience is offered in the research literature. Not all of it will prove helpful to every college and university, but much of can be adapted to almost any institution's individual needs. Cascio (1986, p. 312) suggests that administrators who are serious about improving job performance through appraisal interviews should address certain activities before, during, and after the interviews.

> *Before:* (1) communicate frequently with administrators about their performance, (2) get training in performance appraisal interviewing, (3) plan to use a problem-solving approach rather than "tell-and-sell," (4) encourage administrators to prepare for performance appraisal interviews. *During:* (1) encourage administrator participation, (2) judge performance, not personality and mannerisms, (3) be specific, (4) be an active listener, (5) set mutually agreeable goals for future improvement. *After:* (1) communicate frequently with administrators about their performance, (2) periodically assess progress toward goals, (3) make organizational rewards contingent on performance.

Rice (1985) suggests the following:

1. Determine in advance what you want to achieve or what institutional policy says you should achieve in your performance appraisal interview.
2. Ask fact-finding questions to prompt the administrator to recall examples of good or poor performance.
3. Find out if the administrator believes your ratings are fair.
4. Demonstrate that you care about the administrator as an individual and about his or her career.
5. Always be specific and constructive in your criticism. Use precise and apt examples.
6. Keep the discussion on a professional level.

The *Marist College Review and Planning Evaluation Manual* (1987), developed for use in performance appraisals, includes the following suggestions: (1) devote sufficient time to the interview, (2) encourage the administrator to voice an opinion about the adequacy of supervision, (3) learn the administrator's views on his or her academic position and work load, (4) be ready to reconsider the rating upon presentation of sufficient evidence but not to appease, (5) avoid interruptions during the interview, and (6) ask the administrator to sign the evaluation form.

Brett and Fredian (1981) find that the successful appraisal interview is structured so that both administrator and supervisor approach it as problem solving, not a fault-finding exercise. Discussion of sensitive issues focuses on the deficiency and not on the person. Threat to the administrator's self-esteem should be minimized (Meyer, 1977).

The interview will tend to go better if the administrator reviews his or her performance prior to discussing it with the supervisor. One approach is to hand the administrator a blank form for self-appraisal. During the subsequent interview the self-rating can be compared to ratings by others. Areas of agreement and disagreement can be discussed as well as areas for improvement.

In general, the more the administrator participates positively in the interview, the more fruitful will the interview be in terms of future performance. Perhaps the most critical skill employed by the supervisor is the art of listening, really listening. What the administrator has to say is then restated by the supervisor to be certain that their understanding coincides. Active listening, remarks Sashkin (1981), indicates that the supervisor has heard clearly and understands sympathetically.

Because some supervisors find it very difficult to act simultaneously as judges and coaches in the interview, Cherrington (1987) and Mondy and Noe (1984) recommend splitting the interview in two. One part should concentrate on outcomes and results, the other on behaviors and personal development. As a matter of practice, few colleges and universities conduct two separate interviews. The extra time required and the overall discomfort with the entire concept of appraisal and interview, for administrator and supervisor alike, militate against this approach.

Feedback of Evaluation Results. As a general rule, the administrator being assessed should have ready access to all evaluative information, except that which by previous agreement is to remain confidential. What qualifies as confidential? Personal letters, notes jotted down after discussions, candid interviews, perhaps. There must be a genuinely compelling reason to withhold information as confidential. It must be the rare exception to the policy of full disclosure.

Another general rule is that those who provide information are entitled to feedback of the results of the appraisal. Some institutions restrict a group's feedback. Students and faculty, for example, receive feedback only on their own responses. Other institutions offer full disclosure of all summarized information to all groups, except information that is extremely private or sensitive.

What factors contribute to the decision on how widespread the feedback should be? They include (1) how firm the belief is that administrators are accountable to the governing body, the faculty, students, and nonacademic staff; (2) the visibility of the administrator; (3) how genuinely different campus groups participate in institutional governance; (4) the level of morale at the institution; (5) the level of mutual trust and respect among administrators, faculty members, students, and nonacademic staff.

Conclusion

At bottom, performance appraisal is a feedback process. Research indicates that well-managed feedback may improve performance from 10 to 30 percent (Landy, Farr, and Jacobs, 1982). At its most effective, feedback is a continuing process. To expect administrators to know how well or poorly they are doing without regular feedback from supervisors is fantasy (Walther and Taylor, 1983).

Two final points are worth making. First, there must be

close linkage between performance on the one hand and salary and promotion decisions on the other. If so, administrators will embrace the appraisal system and be content with the results. Second, personal development opportunities should be a direct and natural outgrowth of the performance assessment. Evaluation and professional development should go hand in hand in the ongoing program of institutional improvement.

The next chapter will examine the legal climate for today's academic administrator.

Appendix to Chapter Four
Selected Administrative Evaluation Forms

Exhibit 1. Evaluation of Administrators.

Common Areas for Evaluation

1. Planning and Organization
2. Implementation
3. Efficiency
4. Coordination/Cooperation
5. Collegiality
6. Communication
7. Creativity
8. Professional Growth

Definitions of Ratings

1. *Excellent:* Performance goes well beyond expected standards, and, upon occasion, it adds new dimensions of activity to the position.

2. *Standard:* Performance more than meets minimum requirements of the position but is not up to the individual's capability or the limits of the position.

3. *Needs Greater Emphasis:* Performance is less than expected, less than standard. Supervisor and employee should review job expectations, and the supervisor should provide specific comments when marking this column.

4. *Not Applicable* (NA) These standards of behavior and performance are not expected of this position.

5. *Not Observed* (NO) No opportunity to observe.

Exhibit 1. Evaluation of Administrators, Cont'd.

Directions: Each quality is viewed as a continuum ranging from "Needs Emphasis" to "Excellent." Comments on each area are encouraged.

	Needs Emphasis	STD	EXC	NA	NO
1. Planning and Organization					
a. participates in planning based on a sound understanding of the university's total mission	____	____	____	____	____
b. establishes definite objectives and goals	____	____	____	____	____
c. formulates effective plans to achieve objectives and goals	____	____	____	____	____
d. coordinates planning efforts with other university officials and offices	____		____	____	____

Comments:

	Needs Emphasis	STD	EXC	NA	NO
2. Implementation					
a. has the knowledge necessary to fulfill administrative responsibilities	____	____	____	____	____
b. meets objectives and goals on time	____	____	____	____	____
c. consults with others and makes appropriate referrals	____		____	____	____
d. properly accepts and follows directions	____		____	____	____
e. uses university's resources prudently	____		____	____	____

Comments:

3. Decision Making

	Needs Emphasis	STD	EXC	NA	NO
a. evaluates problems objectively	⸺	⸺	⸺	⸺	⸺
b. reaches decisions effectively without unnecessary delay	⸺	⸺	⸺	⸺	⸺
c. is able to adapt to changing situations	⸺	⸺	⸺	⸺	⸺

Comments:

4. Supervisory Ability

	Needs Emphasis	STD	EXC	NA	NO
a. is sensitive to the needs and abilities of subordinates	⸺	⸺	⸺	⸺	⸺
b. effectively supervises work of subordinates	⸺	⸺	⸺	⸺	⸺
c. properly delegates responsibilities	⸺	⸺	⸺	⸺	⸺
d. helps professional development of subordinates	⸺	⸺	⸺	⸺	⸺

Comments:

5. Communicative Skills

	Needs Emphasis	STD	EXC	NA	NO
a. listens to and communicates well with subordinates, peers, supervisors, and other university constituencies	⸺	⸺	⸺	⸺	⸺
b. contributes effectively to staff discussions and meetings	⸺	⸺	⸺	⸺	⸺
c. produces clear reports and correspondence	⸺	⸺	⸺	⸺	⸺

Comments:

(continued on next page)

Exhibit 1. Evaluation of Administrators, Cont'd.

	Needs Emphasis	STD	EXC	NA	NO
6. Initiative (overall)					
a. shows drive and energy	___	___	___	___	___
b. is innovative in meeting job responsibilities	___	___	___	___	___
c. is willing to work beyond ordinary requirements when necessary	___	___	___	___	___

Comments:

	Needs Emphasis	STD	EXC	NA	NO
7. Professional Self-Improvement					
a. has knowledge of current developments in the field	___	___	___	___	___
b. pursues professional growth opportunities	___	___	___	___	___
c. participates in appropriate professional organizations	___	___	___	___	___

Comments:

8. Overall Value to Division

	Needs Emphasis	STD	EXC	NA	NO
a. understands and contributes to the division's mission	——	——	——	——	——
b. participates willingly and effectively in carrying out staff decisions	——	——	——	——	——
c. represents the division well to outside constituencies	——	——	——	——	——

Comments:

9. Institutional Commitment

	Needs Emphasis	STD	EXC	NA	NO
a. has concern for welfare of total university as well as specific responsibilities	——	——	——	——	——
b. shows interest and involvement in university activities	——	——	——	——	——
c. promotes good public relations	——	——	——	——	——

Comments:

(continued on next page)

Exhibit 1. Evaluation of Administrators, Cont'd.

---

10.   Career Development

Please comment on this individual's potential for career development, if any, within the division and the university:

11.   Other, specific areas of evaluation—for example, risk taking, individual leadership, group leadership, flexibility, adaptability, and tolerance for stress.

A.

B.

C.

D.

E.

Exhibit 1. Evaluation of Administrators, Cont'd.

---

12.   Comments and Recommendations

Summary (check one) _____ Excellent _____ Good _____ Standard

_____ Below Standard

Rater's Signature _____

_____
(Title)

This review has been   Date _____
discussed with me

_____

Date _____

Source: Bucknell University. Reproduced by permission.

Exhibit 2. Administrative Evaluation Report.

Purposes of this evaluation: To make an evaluative inventory indicating strengths and weaknesses and to outline a practical improvement program, if indicated. These evaluations will provide a history of job effectiveness, development, and progress.

_____ _____ _____
(Name) (Department) (Job Title)

_____ _____ _____
(Length of Time in Present Position) (Academic Year) (Date of Report)

Rating Factors: Indicate your rating by considering how this employee is performing on the job. For each category, place a check ☐ in the box over the description which best fits the employee.

1. Job Knowledge Not Observed ☐	☐ Has gaps in fundamental knowledge and skills of the job. (a)	☐ Has satisfactory knowledge and skill for the routine phases of the job. (b)	☐ Has good knowledge and is well skilled in all phases of the job. (c)	☐ Has an exceptional understanding and skill in all phases of the job. (d)	☐ Has a far-reaching grasp of the entire broad job area. Authority in his or her field. (e)
2. Planning Ability Not Observed ☐	☐ Relies on others to bring problems to his or her attention. Often fails to see ahead. (a)	☐ Plans ahead just enough to get by in present job. (b)	☐ Is a careful, effective planner. Anticipates and takes action to solve problems. (c)	☐ Capable of planning beyond requirements of the present job. (d)	☐ Capable of top-level planning of high caliber. (e)
3. Management Ability Not Observed ☐	☐ Is a poor organizer. Does not make effective use of material or man power. (a)	☐ Maintains minimum efficiency of operation. Control could be improved. (b)	☐ Displays efficiency of operation. Makes wise use of material and man power. (c)	☐ Displays very effective organization. Carefully balances methods and results. (d)	☐ Is a highly skilled organizer. Is able to obtain optimum effectiveness. (e)

	(a)	(b)	(c)	(d)	(e)
4. Quality of Leadership ☐ Not Observed	☐ Often weak and unable to exert control. (a)	☐ Normally develops fairly adequate control and direction. (b)	☐ Consistently a good leader. Commands respect of staff. (c)	☐ Exceptional skill in directing others to great effort. (d)	☐ Reflects high-level leadership. (e)
5. Initiative and Creativity ☐ Not Observed	☐ Has little capability for developing new ideas. Often ignores problems. (a)	☐ Has occasionally anticipated problems and developed solutions. (b)	☐ Is usually creative and initiates new procedures. (c)	☐ Always takes the initiative and is exceptionally creative. (d)	☐ Is able to see beyond the limits of own area. Often initiates and is creative for entire college. (e)
6. Executive Judgment ☐ Not Observed	☐ Decisions and recommendations are sometimes unsound or ineffective. (a)	☐ Judgment is usually sound and reasonable with occasional errors. (b)	☐ Displays good judgment resulting from sound evaluation. (c)	☐ An exceptionally sound, logical thinker in situations that occur in his or her area. (d)	☐ Consistently arrives at the right decision even on highly complex matters. (e)
7. Oral and Written Expression ☐ Not Observed	☐ Write ☐ Speak Unable to express thoughts clearly. Lacks organization. (a)	☐ Write ☐ Speak Expresses thoughts satisfactorily on routine matters. (b)	☐ Write ☐ Speak Usually organizes and expresses thoughts clearly and concisely. (c)	☐ Write ☐ Speak Consistently able to express ideas clearly. (d)	☐ Write ☐ Speak Outstanding ability to communicate ideas to others. (e)

(continued on next page)

Exhibit 2. Administrative Evaluation Report, Cont'd.

	(a)	(b)	(c)	(d)	(e)
8. Human Relations ☐ Not Observed	☐ Does not get along well with people. Definitely hinders his or her effectiveness. (a)	☐ Occasional difficulty in getting along with his or her associates. (b)	☐ Gets along with people adequately. Has average skill at maintaining good relations. (c)	☐ Above-average skills in human relations are an asset. (d)	☐ Has outstanding ability in dealing with colleagues. Increases his or her effectiveness. (e)
9. Dependability ☐ Not Observed	☐ Definitely unreliable and unable to carry out work independently. (a)	☐ Can normally be expected to fulfill assignments with some supervision. (b)	☐ Consistently dependable in working toward established goals. (c)	☐ Exceptionally dependable and meets goals within established deadlines. (d)	☐ Outstandingly dependable and works independently with effectiveness. (e)
10. Delegation of Responsibility ☐ Not Observed	☐ Does not delegate responsibility and performs even minor tasks himself. (a)	☐ Is reluctant to delegate responsibility but occasionally allows staff to assume some. (b)	☐ Usually delegates appropriate responsibility to his or her staff. (c)	☐ Effectively delegates appropriate responsibility to his or her staff. (d)	☐ Highly skilled in delegating responsibility and encourages his or her staff to grow in responsibility. (e)
11. Service to College and Community ☐ Not Observed	☐ Does not involve him- or herself in service to college and community. (a)	☐ Occasionally contributes to the benefit of the college and community. (b)	☐ Has contributed measurably in service to both college and community. (c)	☐ Has rendered consistent service to college and community. (d)	☐ His or her service to the college and community is a definite asset and deserves recognition. (e)

Exhibit 2. Administrative Evaluation Report, Cont'd.

Overall Evaluation of Performance in Present Position

☐   ☐   ☐   ☐   ☐

Unsatisfac-   Less than   Effective   Highly   Outstanding
tory   Fully   and   Effective
           Effective   Competent

Supportive Comments: (Must be completed, giving specific facts, weakness/
achievements.)

Recommendations for Development: (Must be completed for overall evaluations, achievements.)

Evaluating
Official: Signature _____ Title_____ Date_____

This evaluation report has been reviewed by me, and I make the following
comments:

Evaluatee: Signature _____ Date _____

Comments by Dean of Instructional Services:

Dean of Instruc-
tional Services: Signature _____ Date _____

Action Taken by Academic Vice-President:

Academic
Vice-President: Signature _____ Date _____

Exhibit 3. Evaluation of the Dean: Faculty Survey.

Department _____ Rank _____ Sex: M___ F___

Directions: Please respond to the items below in two ways. First, indicate your sense of the *importance* of each characteristic, using the following scale:

1 = Not at all important
2 = Slightly important
3 = Moderately important
4 = Very important
5 = Absolutely important

Second, rate the dean's *performance* of the characteristic, using the following scale:

1 = Not at all descriptive of the dean
2 = Slightly descriptive
3 = Moderately descriptive
4 = Very descriptive
5 = Absolutely descriptive of the dean

Please rate *all* "importance" items. If you feel you have not had sufficient contact to judge "performance," mark the column labeled X.

Please read all items prior to rating.

Important?						Item	Descriptive?					
Not at all	Slightly	Moderately	Very	Absolutely			Not at all	Slightly	Moderately	Very	Absolutely	Cannot judge
1	2	3	4	5		1. Communicates her position on college priorities.	1	2	3	4	5	X
1	2	3	4	5		2. Is open to divergent points of view.	1	2	3	4	5	X
1	2	3	4	5		3. Is accessible to individual faculty members.	1	2	3	4	5	X
1	2	3	4	5		4. Supports working relationships among departments.	1	2	3	4	5	X
1	2	3	4	5		5. Maintains positive working relationships with department chairs.	1	2	3	4	5	X
1	2	3	4	5		6. Communicates her expectations of individual departments.	1	2	3	4	5	X
1	2	3	4	5		7. Interacts with faculty members in a professional manner.	1	2	3	4	5	X
1	2	3	4	5		8. Makes wise recommendations regarding promotion and tenure.	1	2	3	4	5	X
1	2	3	4	5		9. Fairly evaluates faculty performance when making salary decisions.	1	2	3	4	5	X
1	2	3	4	5		10. Maintains an effective group of assistant/associate deans and administrative staff.	1	2	3	4	5	X
1	2	3	4	5		11. Maintains an effective group of department chairs.	1	2	3	4	5	X
1	2	3	4	5		12. Addresses problems related to productivity of tenured faculty.	1	2	3	4	5	X
1	2	3	4	5		13. Maintains a balance between departmental autonomy and the dean's office in decisions that affect departments.	1	2	3	4	5	X
1	2	3	4	5		14. Involves faculty in setting policies for the college.	1	2	3	4	5	X
1	2	3	4	5		15. Exercises good judgment in the allocation of resources within the college.	1	2	3	4	5	X
1	2	3	4	5		16. Grasps the diverse needs of the disciplines that constitute the college.	1	2	3	4	5	X

(continued on next page)

Exhibit 3. Evaluation of the Dean: Faculty Survey, Cont'd.

Important?					#		Descriptive?					
Not at all	Slightly	Moderately	Very	Absolutely			Not at all	Slightly	Moderately	Very	Absolutely	Cannot judge
1	2	3	4	5	17.	Handles problems decisively.	1	2	3	4	5	X
1	2	3	4	5	18.	Makes decisions that reflect a thorough understanding of the issues involved.	1	2	3	4	5	X
1	2	3	4	5	19.	Provides information on actions taken to all concerned.	1	2	3	4	5	X
1	2	3	4	5	20.	Follows through on recommendations of department evaluators or accreditors.	1	2	3	4	5	X
1	2	3	4	5	21.	Creates an atmosphere conducive to high faculty performance.	1	2	3	4	5	X
1	2	3	4	5	22.	Sets realistic goals for the college.	1	2	3	4	5	X
1	2	3	4	5	23.	Appropriately emphasizes teaching excellence.	1	2	3	4	5	X
1	2	3	4	5	24.	Appropriately emphasizes excellence in research.	1	2	3	4	5	X
1	2	3	4	5	25.	Appropriately emphasizes excellence in service.	1	2	3	4	5	X
1	2	3	4	5	26.	Assists faculty in obtaining grants.	1	2	3	4	5	X
1	2	3	4	5	27.	Encourages collaboration among the various schools of the university.	1	2	3	4	5	X
1	2	3	4	5	28.	Is a successful advocate at the university level in competing for resources.	1	2	3	4	5	X
1	2	3	4	5	29.	Is an effective leader.	1	2	3	4	5	X
1	2	3	4	5	30.	Communicates to the university the value of a liberal education.	1	2	3	4	5	X
1	2	3	4	5	31.	Represents the views of the college faculty to the university.	1	2	3	4	5	X
1	2	3	4	5	32.	Advances the college's undergraduate programs.	1	2	3	4	5	X
1	2	3	4	5	33.	Advances the college's graduate programs.	1	2	3	4	5	X
1	2	3	4	5	34.	Balances the various aspects of her job.	1	2	3	4	5	X
1	2	3	4	5	35.	Helps protect academic freedom.	1	2	3	4	5	X
1	2	3	4	5	36.	Is an advocate for affirmative action issues.	1	2	3	4	5	X
1	2	3	4	5	37.	Has the political savvy to get things done.	1	2	3	4	5	X
1	2	3	4	5	38.	Gets things done.	1	2	3	4	5	X

Exhibit 3. Evaluation of the Dean: Faculty Survey, Cont'd.

Written Comments

Department _____ Rank_____ Sex M___F ___

A.   If you would like to elaborate on a response given to any item(s) in this survey, please do so below (please refer to specific item numbers).

B.   What is your overall evaluation of the dean's performance?

C.   If you could make one or two recommendations to the dean that would most improve her effectiveness, what would they be?

Source: College of Humanities and Sciences, Virginia Commonwealth University. Reproduced by permission.

Exhibit 4. Diagnostic Checklist.

	True		Half true	False		Not applicable	Applicable, but don't know
	True	More true than false	Half true	More false than true	False	Not applicable	Applicable, but don't know
	1	2	3	4	5	6	7
1. Rigid and inflexible in interpreting rules and regulations.							
2. Prejudiced or biased for and against certain programs.							
3. Prejudiced or biased for and against certain faculty members.							
4. Difficult to communicate with.							
5. Indiscreet.							
6. Lacks courage.							
7. Blames higher-ups for unpopular decisions.							
8. Does not delegate anything.							
9. Always delegates everything.							
10. Lazy.							
11. Does not follow through on things.							
12. Does not submit reports on time or meet deadlines.							
13. Does not involve faculty members in decision making.							
14. Uses poor judgment in personnel decisions.							
15. Provides poor support documentation for those recommended for tenure and promotion.							
16. Has not developed a long-range plan for the department.							
17. Does not follow a long-range plan that has been developed.							

Exhibit 4. Diagnostic Checklist, Cont'd.

	True			False			
	True	More true than false	Half true	More false than true	False	Not applicable	Applicable, but don't know
	1	2	3	4	5	6	7
18. Does not become personally involved in evaluating faculty performance—depends completely on a committee for this function.							
19. Does not establish department priorities for expenditure of faculty time and effort.							
20. Does not establish department priorities for expenditure of department budget.							
21. Poor advocate for the department.							
22. Creates conflict among faculty members.							
23. Unwilling to take any action without first checking with the dean.							
24. Cannot make up his or her mind and changes each decision several times.							
25. Afraid to confront faculty members who are violating a college regulation, missing classes, or not living up to their teaching responsibilities.							
26. Cultivates close social and professional relationships with higher-level administrators to whom the dean reports and uses the relationships to circumvent the dean.							
27. Has played the squeeze-game on the dean to extract additional funds for the department budget.							

(continued on next page)

Exhibit 4. Diagnostic Checklist, Cont'd.

| | True | | | False | | | |
	True	More true than false	Half true	More false than true	False	Not applicable	Applicable, but don't know
	1	2	3	4	5	6	7
28. Has played the squeeze-game on the dean to extract an additional faculty position for the department.							
29. Has funds left in the departmental budget at the end of the fiscal year and spends those funds hurriedly and in an unplanned manner.							
30. Does not keep the dean informed on what is going on in the department.							
31. Does not personally make a decision—always depends on a departmental committee to make a recommendation which is followed without challenge.							
32. Passes departmental problems to the dean for resolution.							
33. Unfamiliar with university and college rules and regulations and, because of this, sometimes violates those rules and regulations.							
34. Knowingly violates regulations and rules, thus creating problems for the dean.							
35. Uses poor judgment in determining for which existing regulations and rules exceptions might be made.							
36. Takes pride in never doing paper work.							
37. Asks for more resources from the dean than the dean has to give—is insensitive to the total amount of resources that the dean has available for distribution.							

Exhibit 4. Diagnostic Checklist, Cont'd.

	True			False			
	True	More true than false	Half true	More false than true	False	Not applicable	Applicable, but don't know
	1	2	3	4	5	6	7
38. Asks the dean to make decisions for which the dean does not have final authority.							
39. Makes promises to the dean, faculty, and students that are never kept.							
40. Does not express an interest in or does nothing to develop programs for professional growth of faculty members.							
41. Unwilling or unable to give non-academic support staff clear, precise instructions on what they are expected to do.							
42. Seldom available to meet with students.							
43. Seldom available to meet with faculty.							
44. Spends considerable time traveling off campus and is thus personally unavailable to provide the department with adequate leadership.							
45. Spends considerable time on projects not directly related to the management and leadership of the department, and is thus unavailable to provide the department with adequate leadership.							

Source: The Academic Dean: Dove, Dragon, and Diplomat, by A. Tucker and R. Bryan, © 1987 by American Council on Education/Macmillan Publishing Co. Reprinted by permission.

Exhibit 5. General Purpose Questionnaire for Evaluating Academic Administrators.

Instructions: This evaluation consists of thirty-seven questions. Please read each statement carefully. Mark one of the six alternatives for each statement:

    (1)   Strongly agree
    (2)   Agree
    (3)   Neutral (on balance, not sure)
    (4)   Disagree
    (5)   Strongly disagree
    (NA)   Not applicable

If you think you have insufficient data to evaluate any question, do not answer that question.

A. Leadership

1. _____ Reflects the characteristics of a generally well-informed and broadly educated person who is aware of problems and issues in higher education.

2. _____ Supports experimentation, research, and publication.

3. _____ Demonstrates initiative in the improvement and development of the unit for which responsible.

4. _____ Invests time and effort in the development and improvement of the university as a whole.

5. _____ Has the confidence and respect of others.

6. _____ Maintains confidentiality in relationships.

7. _____ Functions effectively under pressure.

8. _____ Is skillful at handling difficult situations involving people.

9. _____ Displays no favoritism.

10. _____ Is productive in accomplishing administrative goals and objectives.

B. Administration

11. _____ Assigns duties and tasks clearly.

12. _____ Distributes assignments allowing sufficient time for completion of the tasks.

13. _____ Delegates authority where appropriate.

14. _____ Follows through on commitments.

15. _____ Establishes reasonable goals.

16. _____ Makes suitable progress toward goals.

17. _____ Is a good financial manager.

**Exhibit 5. General Purpose Questionnaire for Evaluating
Academic Administrators, Cont'd.**

18. _____ Carries out the policies and procedures of the university correctly.

19. _____ Is skillful at recruiting new personnel and/or promoting recruitment.

20. _____ Provides and/or promotes adequate orientation for new personnel to university policies and procedures.

21. _____ Engenders an enthusiastic and optimistic attitude in the unit.

22. _____ Facilitates the work of others.

23. _____ Encourages high-quality work.

24. _____ Works well with other administrators.

25. _____ Manages his or her office and its paper work well.

26. _____ Bases decisions on objective data or criteria whenever possible.

27. _____ Assumes responsibility for his or her decisions or actions.

28. _____ Supports affirmative action efforts within his or her unit.

C. *Communications*

29. _____ Is available for consultation.

30. _____ Respects diverse opinions and ideas.

31. _____ Understands the needs of others.

32. _____ Effectively represents those in his or her unit to superiors and the rest of the university.

33. _____ Promotes the unit to the community outside of the university.

34. _____ Reinforces unit members when they deserve reinforcement.

35. _____ Reprimands unit members when they deserve reprimands.

36. _____ Has a helpful attitude toward students.

D. *Overall Evaluation of the Administrator*

37. _____ This person is an effective administrator.

Please add comments concerning the administrator below. Attach a separate sheet if necessary.

Exhibit 6. Provost's Review.
Southeast Missouri State University (SEMO).

Position/Rank	Years at SEMO	College/Unit
☐ Instructor	☐ 1 to 2	☐ Business/Public adm.
☐ Assistant professor	☐ 3 to 4	☐ Education/Behavioral sci.
☐ Associate professor	☐ 5 to 6	☐ Humanities
☐ Professor	☐ 7 to 8	☐ Science/Technology
☐ Administrator	☐ 9 to 10	☐ Social science
☐ Staff	☐ 11 to 12	☐ Kent Library
☐ Other	☐ More than 12	☐ Other

University service role (last 4 yrs.)	Contact with the provost (last 4 yrs.)
☐ Member academic council	☐ Infrequent
☐ Member faculty senate	☐ On committee with provost
☐ Department chairperson	☐ On committee chaired by provost
☐ College dean	☐ Committee chair with provost member
☐ Vice-president	☐ In my role as a university admin.
☐ Position outside SEMO	☐ As a person from outside SEMO
☐ None of the above	☐ None of the above

Performance

Importance

Please select the five to seven factors you regard as most important and least important to the provost's role.

        7 6 5 4 3 2 1   + −

1. ☐☐☐☐☐☐☐	32.	☐☐	Administrative management
2. ☐☐☐☐☐☐☐		☐☐	Executive judgment
3. ☐☐☐☐☐☐☐		☐☐	Delegating authority and responsibility
4. ☐☐☐☐☐☐☐		☐☐	Providing academic leadership
5. ☐☐☐☐☐☐☐		☐☐	Acting decisively
6. ☐☐☐☐☐☐☐		☐☐	Planning ability
7. ☐☐☐☐☐☐☐		☐☐	Encourage faculty's professional development
8. ☐☐☐☐☐☐☐		☐☐	Improvement of teaching
9. ☐☐☐☐☐☐☐		☐☐	Role as a faculty representative
10. ☐☐☐☐☐☐☐		☐☐	Effectiveness attract/retain quality faculty
11. ☐☐☐☐☐☐☐		☐☐	Keeping communication lines open
12. ☐☐☐☐☐☐☐		☐☐	Providing academic freedom
13. ☐☐☐☐☐☐☐		☐☐	Skill in working with groups
14. ☐☐☐☐☐☐☐		☐☐	Communicating ideas
15. ☐☐☐☐☐☐☐		☐☐	Sensitivity to faculty concerns
16. ☐☐☐☐☐☐☐		☐☐	Handling conflict
17. ☐☐☐☐☐☐☐		☐☐	Introduction and acceptance of new ideas

Exhibit 6. Provost's Review.
Southeast Missouri State University (SEMO), Cont'd.

	Performance	Importance	
	7 6 5 4 3 2 1	+ −	
18.	☐☐☐☐☐☐☐	☐☐	Availability to faculty
19.	☐☐☐☐☐☐☐	☐☐	Listening to faculty
20.	☐☐☐☐☐☐☐	☐☐	Honesty
21.	☐☐☐☐☐☐☐	☐☐	Personal/professional stability
22.	☐☐☐☐☐☐☐	☐☐	Fairness
23.	☐☐☐☐☐☐☐	☐☐	Role as a university representative
24.	☐☐☐☐☐☐☐	☐☐	Role as a scholar
25.	☐☐☐☐☐☐☐	☐☐	Commitment to collegiality: seeks advice
26.	☐☐☐☐☐☐☐	☐☐	Commitment to collegiality: recommendations
27.	☐☐☐☐☐☐☐	☐☐	Commitment to collegiality: reason nonsupport
28.	☐☐☐☐☐☐☐	☐☐	Standards and expectations
29.	☐☐☐☐☐☐☐	☐☐	Academic excellence
30.	☐☐☐☐☐☐☐	☐☐	Evaluation/review of acad. programs/policies
31.	☐☐☐☐☐☐☐	☐☐	Overall rating

33. The best thing about the provost or his office is:

34. The worst thing about the provost or his office is:

35. The president will meet with a group if a majority of the group requests a meeting. Do you wish the president to meet with your group for additional input?

Yes   No   (Circle one)

Source: Southeast Missouri State University. Reprinted by permission.

Exhibit 7. Administrative Review Questionnaire.

Instructions for completing the questionnaire: It will take you approximately twenty to thirty minutes to complete this questionnaire. We suggest you quickly review the entire questionnaire first, and then begin to respond to the questions. When you answer the questionnaire, we hope you will respond specifically in those areas where your knowledge of the performance of the administrator is best. Leave the questions blank where you have limited or no knowledge.

Part I: Background of Respondent

Please check the appropriate categories below:

A. I am a (an):
    (check the *one* that *best* fits)

    ____ Administrator

    ____ Faculty member

    ____ Department chair or program coordinator

    ____ Staff member

    ____ Student

    ____ Off-campus respondent

    ____ Other (explain) _____

B. I have worked with this administrator:
    (check the *one* that *best* fits)

    ____ less than one year

    ____ one to five years

    ____ five years or more

Part II: Evaluation of the Administrator in Areas Common to All Administrators

In this section of the questionnaire the administrator is to be reviewed in the categories of Leadership, Management, Decision Making, Communication, and Professional Development. Under each category are a series of statements that describe characteristics of administrative work. These are listed to help you focus on elements that you should consider within each specific category. After the statements, space is provided for you to *describe* your perception of the administrator's effectiveness *within that category.* Please be as candid in your comments as possible. Use specific examples whenever possible. If you need additional space use the back of the sheet.

Exhibit 7. Administrative Review Questionnaire, Cont'd.

A. Leadership

- Maintains positive and productive relationship with appropriate individuals within the academic community, that is, with faculty, staff, administrators, students. Treats all individuals fairly and with respect.
- Provides adequate information on a timely basis. Gives clear directions and constructive feedback to those reporting to her or him.
- Provides opportunities for leadership development for subordinates. Stimulates others to become involved and accept responsibility.
- Demonstrates vision and long-range planning.
- Demonstrates perseverance in dealing with obstacles, pursuing new challenges, and working through the bureaucracy.
- Demonstrates initiative. Sets and strives to attain appropriate goals.

Comments (be specific):

B. Management

- Demonstrates knowledge of the university system, policies, and practices and applies them appropriately. Demonstrates careful planning and ability to meet deadlines.
- Gives recognition to individuals who warrant it. Makes reasonable demands, sets reasonable standards and goals. Makes effective use of staff. Delegates authority and follows up on the delegation.
- Plans ahead. Anticipates changing needs and circumstances. Demonstrates responsiveness to changing policies, procedures, and information overload.
- Demonstrates willingness to put in the time and effort necessary for quality work.
- Makes effective use of and fairly allocates all resources (personnel, money, equipment, space).

Comments (be specific):

(continued on next page)

Exhibit 7. Administrative Review Questionnaire, Cont'd.

C. Decision Making

- Demonstrates the ability to make decisions and exercises good judgment.
- Involves others in decisions that affect them. Consults fully with appropriate individuals, committees, and groups before reaching final decisions.
- Demonstrates creativity and flexibility in decision making. Explores all problems objectively, considering implications and alternatives before making timely decisions.
- Demonstrates consistent follow-up on decisions once made.

Comments (be specific):

D. Communication

- Demonstrates effective verbal communication skills with appropriate individuals and groups on campus.
- Demonstrates the ability to listen effectively and maintains a reasonable open-door policy for communication purposes.
- Demonstrates effective written communication skills.
- Builds positive relationships through open communication with external groups and agencies including the media, community, and alumni.

Comments (be specific):

E. Professional Development

- Remains abreast of developments in higher education in general with an emphasis upon the area of the administrator's responsibility.
- Retains currency in her or his discipline by participating in appropriate professional activities such as memberships and leadership positions in professional organizations, conference and workshop attendance, occasional teaching, lecturing, or consulting.
- Continues with professional study, research, or creative endeavors that result in presentations, written reports or research, and so on, consistent with the time and energy demands of the position.

Comments (be specific):

Exhibit 7. Administrative Review Questionnaire, Cont'd.

Part III: Overall Performance Rating

After reviewing your responses in Part II, please give an overall rating of the performance of this administrator.

_____ 1. Excellent—Outstanding

_____ 2. Good—Strong

_____ 3. Average—Adequate

_____ 4. Poor—Weak

_____ 5. Unsatisfactory

Comments:

For this questionnaire to be used as part of the Administrative Review data, please print your name and sign below:

_____   _____
            (Print Name)   (Signature)

Part IV: Evaluation of the Administrator in Specific Job
*   Assignments (Optional)*

These specific job assignments were developed by the Review Committee and the administrator using his or her job description. Please check those areas where you have knowledge of the administrator's performance and comment upon them in the space provided.

_____ 1. Membership or role on specific committee—for example, Academic Senate Committee, Equipment Committee, School Council, and so on.

_____ 2. Specific assignments or commitments—for example, space allocation, major curriculum revision, major facility planning, and so on.

_____ 3. Specific external assignments or commitments—for example, fund raising, conference planning, community projects.

For this questionnaire to be used as part of the Administrative Review data, please print your name and sign below:

_____   _____
            (Print Name)   (Signature)

Note: This questionnaire is in the developmental stage and is still undergoing field testing.

Source: San Francisco State University. Reproduced by permission.

Exhibit 8. Chairperson Information Form and Survey Form.

Decad

CHAIRPERSON INFORMATION FORM

for use with the Decad Survey Form

Name _____   (Initials) _____   (1-20)

Department _____   (21-39)
(40-43)

Institution _____

Number of faculty asked to respond _____   (44-46)

Approximately what percentage of the faculty in this department is tenured?   (47)
(1) Over 80%   (2) 60-79%   (3) 40-59%   (4) Under 40%

Are members of the department housed: (48)
(1) In a single building?   (2) In more than one building?

How many formal department faculty meetings were called in the past 12 months?   (49)
(1) None   (2) 1 or 2   (3) 3-5   (4) 6-9   (5) 10 or more

How many years have you served as chairperson/head of this department?   (50)
(1) This is my first year.   (2) 1-2 years   (3) 3-5 years   (4) 6 or more years

What are the terms of your appointment?   (51)
(1) I was appointed by   (2) I was elected by   (3) I was elected by the
    the dean and serve   the faculty for   faculty but not for
    at his/her pleasure   a specific term   a specific term

- **The list below describes responsibilities which some department chairpersons/heads pursue. Circle the number which describes your judgment of how important each of these is in your role as chairperson/head:**

1 — Not Important   2 — Only So-So   3 — Fairly Important
4 — Quite Important   5 — Essential

CHAIRPERSON/HEAD RESPONSIBILITIES

	RATING	
1. Guides the development of sound procedures for assessing faculty performance.	1 2 3 4 5	(52)
2. Recognizes and rewards faculty in accordance with their contributions to the department's program	1 2 3 4 5	(53)
3. Guides development of sound organizational plan to accomplish departmental program	1 2 3 4 5	(54)
4. Arranges effective and equitable allocation of faculty responsibilities such as committee assignments, teaching loads, etc.	1 2 3 4 5	(55)
5. Takes lead in recruitment of promising faculty	1 2 3 4 5	(56)
6. Fosters good teaching in the department	1 2 3 4 5	(57)
7. Stimulates research and scholarly activity in the department	1 2 3 4 5	(58)
8. Guides curriculum development	1 2 3 4 5	(59)
9. Maintains faculty morale by reducing, resolving, or preventing conflicts	1 2 3 4 5	(60)
10. Fosters development of each faculty member's special talents or interests.	1 2 3 4 5	(61)
11. Understands and communicates expectations of the campus administration to the faculty	1 2 3 4 5	(62)
12. Effectively communicates the department's needs (personnel, space, monetary) to the dean	1 2 3 4 5	(63)
13. Facilitates obtaining grants and contracts from extramural sources	1 2 3 4 5	(64)
14. Improves the department's image and reputation in the total campus community	1 2 3 4 5	(65)
15. Encourages an appropriate balance among specializations within the department	1 2 3 4 5	(66)

(continued on next page)

Exhibit 8. Chairperson Information Form and Survey Form, Cont'd.

Decad

SURVEY FORM--FACULTY REACTIONS TO CHAIRPERSON ACTIVITIES

Department _____ Institution _____

• The list below describes 15 responsibilities which some department chairpersons/heads pursue. In Column 1, circle the number corresponding to your judgment of how important each of these should be for your chairperson/head using the following code:

1 — Not Important   3 — Fairly Important   4 — Quite Important
2 — Only So-So   5 — Essential

• Use Column 2 to describe how effectively you feel your department chairperson/head fulfilled each responsibility during the past 12 months. Omit any item if you feel you cannot make a valid judgment; otherwise circle the number best corresponding to your estimate:

1 — Poor   3 — In Between   4 — Good
2 — Only So-So   5 — Outstanding

IMPORTANCE COLUMN 1	CHAIRPERSON/HEAD RESPONSIBILITIES	PERFORMANCE COLUMN 2
1. 1 2 3 4 5	Guides the development of sound procedures for assessing faculty performance	16. 1 2 3 4 5
2. 1 2 3 4 5	Recognizes and rewards faculty in accordance with their contributions to department's program	17. 1 2 3 4 5
3. 1 2 3 4 5	Guides development of sound organizational plan to accomplish departmental program	18. 1 2 3 4 5
4. 1 2 3 4 5	Arranges effective and equitable allocation of faculty responsibilities such as committee assignments, teaching loads, etc.	19. 1 2 3 4 5
5. 1 2 3 4 5	Takes lead in recruitment of promising faculty.	20. 1 2 3 4 5
6. 1 2 3 4 5	Fosters good teaching in the department	21. 1 2 3 4 5

7.	Stimulates research and scholarly activity in the department	1	2	3	4	5
8.	Guides curriculum development	1	2	3	4	5
9.	Maintains faculty morale by reducing, resolving or preventing conflicts	1	2	3	4	5
10.	Fosters development of each faculty member's special talents or interests	1	2	3	4	5
11.	Understands and communicates expectations of the campus administration to the faculty	1	2	3	4	5
12.	Effectively communicates the department's needs (personnel, space, monetary) to the dean	1	2	3	4	5
13.	Facilitates obtaining grants and contracts from extramural sources	1	2	3	4	5
14.	Improves the department's image and reputation in the total campus community	1	2	3	4	5
15.	Encourages an appropriate balance among academic specializations within the department	1	2	3	4	5

• **Indicate how frequently each of the following 30 statements is descriptive of your department chairperson/head by circling the number corresponding to your judgment:**

1 — Hardly Ever (not at all descriptive)	3 — About Half the Time	4 — More than Half the Time
2 — Less than Half the Time		5 — Almost Always (very descriptive)

The department chairperson/head:

31.	Makes own attitudes clear to the faculty	1	2	3	4	5
32.	Tries out new ideas with the faculty	1	2	3	4	5
33.	Works without a plan	1	2	3	4	5
34.	Maintains definite standards of performance	1	2	3	4	5
35.	Makes sure his/her part in the department is understood by all members	1	2	3	4	5
36.	Lets faculty members know what's expected of them	1	2	3	4	5
37.	Sees to it that faculty members are working up to capacity	1	2	3	4	5
38.	Sees to it that the work of faculty members is coordinated	1	2	3	4	5
39.	Does little things that make it pleasant to be a member of the faculty	1	2	3	4	5
40.	Is easy to understand	1	2	3	4	5
41.	Keeps to him/herself	1	2	3	4	5
42.	Looks out for the personal welfare of individual faculty members	1	2	3	4	5
43.	Refuses to explain actions	1	2	3	4	5
44.	Acts without consulting the faculty	1	2	3	4	5
45.	Is slow to accept new ideas	1	2	3	4	5

22.	1	2	3	4	5
23.	1	2	3	4	5
24.	1	2	3	4	5
25.	1	2	3	4	5
26.	1	2	3	4	5
27.	1	2	3	4	5
28.	1	2	3	4	5
29.	1	2	3	4	5
30.	1	2	3	4	5

(continued on next page)

Exhibit 8. Chairperson Information Form and Survey Form, Cont'd.

46. Treats all faculty members as his/her equal	1	2	3	4	5
47. Is willing to make changes	1	2	3	4	5
48. Makes faculty members feel at ease when talking to them	1	2	3	4	5
49. Puts faculty suggestions into action	1	2	3	4	5
50. Gets faculty approval on important matters before going ahead	1	2	3	4	5
51. Postpones decisions unnecessarily	1	2	3	4	5
52. Is more a reactor than an initiator	1	2	3	4	5
53. Makes it clear that faculty suggestions for improving the department are welcome	1	2	3	4	5
54. Is responsive to one "clique" in the faculty but largely ignores those who are not members of the clique	1	2	3	4	5
55. In expectations of faculty members, makes allowance for their personal or situational problems	1	2	3	4	5
56. Lets faculty members know when they've done a good job	1	2	3	4	5
57. Explains the basis for his/her decisions	1	2	3	4	5
58. Gains input from faculty on important matters	1	2	3	4	5
59. Acts as though visible department accomplishments were vital to him/her	1	2	3	4	5
60. Acts as though high faculty morale was vital to him/her	1	2	3	4	5

● Questions 61-70 ask about yourself or the department in general. Use this answer code:

1 — Definitely False	3 — In Between	5 — Definitely True
2 — More False than True	4 — More True than False	

61. I enjoy my work in this department	1	2	3	4	5
62. I have a positive relationship with the department chairperson	1	2	3	4	5
63. I agree with the priorities and emphases which have guided recent development in the department	1	2	3	4	5
64. The department has been getting stronger in recent years (use responses 1 or 2 if it has been getting weaker; use response 3 if there has been little change)	1	2	3	4	5

During the past 12 months, the department chairperson's/head's effectiveness has been seriously impaired by:

65. Enrollment/retrenchment problems in the department 1 2 3 4 5
66. Inadequate facilities for the department 1 2 3 4 5
67. Bureaucratic requirements and regulations 1 2 3 4 5
68. Inadequate financial resources to support departmental programs 1 2 3 4 5
69. A relatively low priority given to the department by the chairperson's /head's immediate superior 1 2 3 4 5
70. Obstructionism/negativism from one or more senior members of the faculty 1 2 3 4 5

> • **Your responses to the following questions will be returned to your chairperson/head. If you are concerned about anonymity, you may wish to type your responses or have them typed.**

Which matters need priority attention in the department during the next year or two? _____

_____

_____

Identify any departmental policies or procedures which you feel need immediate improvement. _____

_____

_____

What is the most important observation you can make about the department chairperson's/head's:

a) administrative effectiveness? _____

_____

b) administrative style? _____

_____

Other comments: _____

_____

Source: © Center for Faculty Evaluation and Development, Kansas State University. Reprinted by permission.

Exhibit 9. Administrative Review.

The following set of questions has been designed to provide faculty and/or staff with the opportunity to objectively review and rate the performance of administrators. Sufficient space for comments is also provided.

The questionnaire is divided into four categories: Management Style, Leadership, Relationship with Faculty/Staff, and Personal Attributes. Because the questions have been grouped into these four categories, there are some questions that overlap. The last question in each category seeks an *overall* or *general* rating of the performance in the category.

Please rate each question in the four categories using the scale of 1 (Low) to 7 (High). Since this is a general scale designed to be used for several administrators, you may also choose one of two additional options: NA or Unknown. If, for any reason, you feel that a question is inappropriate for a given administrator, use NA.

I. Management Style

	Low 1	2	3	4	5	6	High 7	NA	UNK
1. Accessible									
2. Acts professionally									
3. Consults with others as necessary									
4. Uses reasonable judgment in decisions									
5. Adequately answers questions									
6. Gives feedback									
7. Seeks input of others									
8. Stimulates change									
9. Practices shared governance									
10. Demonstrates interest in students									
11. Knowledgeable about job									
12. Accepts advice									
13. Able to delegate as required									
14. Demonstrates evidence of planning									
15. Works well with others									
16. *Overall* rating on Management Style									

Comments:

II. *Leadership*

	Low 1	2	3	4	5	6	High 7	NA	UNK
17. Makes decisions	—	—	—	—	—	—	—	—	—
18. Actively involved in campus affairs	—	—	—	—	—	—	—	—	—
19. Capably represents the campus	—	—	—	—	—	—	—	—	—
20. Actively supports institutional goals	—	—	—	—	—	—	—	—	—
21. Improves campus image	—	—	—	—	—	—	—	—	—
22. Initiates more than reacts	—	—	—	—	—	—	—	—	—
23. Encourages research and scholarly activity	—	—	—	—	—	—	—	—	—
24. Active in fund raising	—	—	—	—	—	—	—	—	—
25. Willing to take risks	—	—	—	—	—	—	—	—	—
26. Visible on campus	—	—	—	—	—	—	—	—	—
27. *Overall* rating on Leadership	—	—	—	—	—	—	—	—	—

Comments:

(continued on next page)

Exhibit 9. Administrative Review, Cont'd.

III. Relationship with Faculty/Staff

Note: In this category please respond to the questions as either a faculty or staff member—that is, circle the word faculty or staff as they appear so there is no confusion regarding your referent.

		Low 1	2	3	4	5	6	High 7	NA	UNK
28.	Sensitive to faculty/staff needs	—	—	—	—	—	—	—	—	—
29.	Attempts to keep faculty/staff informed on pertinent issues	—	—	—	—	—	—	—	—	—
30.	Maintains a professional attitude	—	—	—	—	—	—	—	—	—
31.	Works cooperatively with faculty/staff	—	—	—	—	—	—	—	—	—
32.	Facilitates work of faculty/staff	—	—	—	—	—	—	—	—	—
33.	Fosters faculty/staff development	—	—	—	—	—	—	—	—	—
34.	Advocate of faculty/staff	—	—	—	—	—	—	—	—	—
35.	Keeps lines of communication open	—	—	—	—	—	—	—	—	—
36.	Solicits input from faculty/staff	—	—	—	—	—	—	—	—	—
37.	Committed to academic values	—	—	—	—	—	—	—	—	—
38.	*Overall* rating on Relationship with Faculty/Staff	—	—	—	—	—	—	—	—	—

Comments:

IV. Personal Attributes

	Low 1	2	3	4	5	6	High 7	NA	UNK
39. Fair and impartial	—	—	—	—	—	—	—	—	—
40. Courteous	—	—	—	—	—	—	—	—	—
41. Communicates clearly and effectively	—	—	—	—	—	—	—	—	—
42. Listens to others	—	—	—	—	—	—	—	—	—
43. Helpful	—	—	—	—	—	—	—	—	—
44. Demonstrates integrity	—	—	—	—	—	—	—	—	—
45. Prompt	—	—	—	—	—	—	—	—	—
46. Accurate	—	—	—	—	—	—	—	—	—
47. Well-organized	—	—	—	—	—	—	—	—	—
48. Committed to scholarship	—	—	—	—	—	—	—	—	—
49. Works well under pressure	—	—	—	—	—	—	—	—	—
50. Open-minded	—	—	—	—	—	—	—	—	—
51. Flexible when necessary	—	—	—	—	—	—	—	—	—
52. Receptive to new ideas	—	—	—	—	—	—	—	—	—
53. Innovative	—	—	—	—	—	—	—	—	—
54. Sympathetic and understanding of others	—	—	—	—	—	—	—	—	—
55. Industrious, hardworking	—	—	—	—	—	—	—	—	—
56. Shows evidence of professional growth	—	—	—	—	—	—	—	—	—
57. *Overall* rating on Personal Attributes	—	—	—	—	—	—	—	—	—

Comments:

Source: The Pennsylvania State University, Beaver Campus. Reproduced by permission.

Exhibit 10. Faculty Evaluation of the Academic Dean.

Please answer each question as fully as possible. Use the reverse side if necessary to complete your statements.

1. What do you consider to be the three most important current tasks of the academic dean at this institution?

a.

b.

c.

2. How well do you think the dean has addressed these tasks?

a.

b.

c.

3. Each faculty member has certain expectations of the dean with regard to the areas of his responsibility. Please evaluate the dean's work this year with respect to meeting your expectations in the following areas:

	Exceeds expectations	Meets expectations	Does not meet expectations	Cannot comment
a. Academic program management	___	___	___	___
b. Academic program leadership	___	___	___	___
c. Faculty personnel matters	___	___	___	___
d. Relating to individual faculty	___	___	___	___
e. Representation of faculty in administrative councils	___	___	___	___
f. Supervision of support organization	___	___	___	___
g. Relating to students	___	___	___	___
h. Relating to off-campus groups	___	___	___	___
i. Commitment to college mission	___	___	___	___
j. _____ (other)	___	___	___	___

Please comment on the back side of this form if you wish to amplify your response to any of the above.

4. Please comment on other information or opinions you feel are pertinent to this assessment.

Exhibit 11. Planning and Assessment Form.

Faculty Member: _____

Chairperson/Dean: _____

I. Planning Conference (Early Winter Quarter)

    A. Statement of institutionally and departmentally related objectives, methods of assessment, and departmental support for this calendar year, including affirmative action efforts (attach additional pages if needed):

    B. Additional Comments

        1. Chairperson's comments:

        2. Faculty member's comments:

We have discussed and agreed upon this statement of objectives, methods of assessment, and departmental support for the current year.

Signature: _____   _____
                (Chairperson)   (Faculty Member)

Date: _____   _____

Exhibit 11. Planning and Assessment Form, Cont'd.

II. Review Conferences

(Optional—may be requested by chairperson or faculty member.)

Changes in the statement of objectives are as follows (date and initial):

III. Final Assessment Conference (Early Winter Quarter)

(*Note:* The same meeting may serve as planning conference for the year ahead.)

Date of Conference: _____

A.   Chairperson's suggestions for the year ahead:

Note: Please forward a copy of this section to Academic Affairs.

Faculty Member: _____ Department: _____ Year: _____

B.   Institutional and departmental responsibilities, including affirmative action efforts, have been discharged through the accomplishment of established objectives as follows:

Faculty member's comments:

Signature: _____   _____
                  (Chairperson)   (Faculty Member)

Date: _____   _____

Source: The University of Tennessee, Martin. Reprinted by permission.

✴ 5 ✴

Ensuring a Sound Legal Basis for Evaluation Activities

Officially, decisions to promote or retain an academic administrator are taken only after a careful weighing of the facts and a
respectful consideration for due process. In the real world, however, such decisions too often are influenced by subjective factors. This is not to say that academic worth goes unrecognized
in personnel decisions but that campus politics and/or personalities too often creep in. This admittedly is regrettable. So is an
evaluation committee member's searching through personnel
files for negative data to support an adverse prejudgment.

Changed Climate

In recent years, however, new forces have been at work in
academia. Decisions to promote or retain an administrator have
been made more public. They are now subject to affirmative action guidelines and court scrutiny. They are no longer left to the
personal discretion of evaluation committee members meeting
behind closed doors. They must be capable of public justification to shield them from lawsuits by the administrator.

What triggered this change? Title VII of the Civil Rights
Act of 1964 prohibited discrimination in employment for reasons of race, color, religion, sex, or national origin. In 1972, an
amendment extended that law's provisions to colleges and uni-

versities. Some institutions tried to avoid liability under Title VII on the basis of their special relationship to a state or church. But their efforts were thwarted by the courts. In *Shawer* v. *Indiana University of Pennsylvania* [602 F. 2d 1161 (3d Cir. 1979)], the United States Court of Appeals for the Third Circuit held that a state university cannot claim exemption from Title VII by invoking the doctrine of the sovereign state's immunity. In *EEOC* v. *Mississippi College* [626 F. 2d 477 (5th Cir. 1980), Cert. Denied, 453 U.S. 912 (1981)], the Court of Appeals for the Fifth Circuit declared that the separation of church and state as guaranteed by the First Amendment does not protect a church-related college from liability under Title VII for unlawful employment practices.

Responding promptly, many institutions of higher education made concerted efforts to hire women and minority members for administrative positions. Now, many of these same institutions appear to be dragging their feet when it comes to promoting women and minority members. And some institutions dismiss them seemingly on a number of pretexts. In addition, sexual harassment has been charged in some cases. In response, a number of women and minority members have filed suits on grounds of discrimination.

The following cases were reported in the *Chronicle of Higher Education* in late 1987:

- Two female staff members sued the University of Vermont, charging that officials retaliated after they complained of sexual harassment by a supervisor. The attorney general of Vermont, whose office investigated the complaint, has joined the suit ("Two Women Staff Members . . . ," 1987).
- A federal district judge has ruled in favor of a black administrator who charged Wayne State University (Michigan) with racial discrimination. The judge ordered university officials to restore the complainant to his job and not to retaliate against him. The complainant charged that he had been forced to quit after university officials harassed him over his views on affirmative action ("Wayne State U. Overruled . . . ," 1987).

- Tennessee State University's former dean of engineering has sued the state's board of regents, contending that he was denied equal pay because of his race and national origin. The suit argues that the former dean, a Nigerian, was paid several thousand dollars less than his counterparts at other engineering schools in the system ("Former Dean Sues . . . ," 1987).

Establishing a Prima Facie Case. Under Title VII, it is not necessary for the aggrieved administrator to prove "intent to discriminate" in order to prove discrimination. The presence of disproportionate numbers of administrators from either a majority or minority group is considered prima facie evidence of discrimination. Any appraisal system leading to such ill balance in promotion or retention of administrators may be discriminatory (Odom, 1977). Another way to establish a prima facie case is to demonstrate that the evaluation criteria were applied unevenly, were biased, or were unconscionably subjective.

Once the administrator establishes a prima facie case, the burden of proof shifts to the institution, which must demonstrate that its decision rests on legitimate grounds in no way prohibited by Title VII. Beckham (1986) points out that it is not the appropriateness of the particular considerations of administrative performance that is challenged. What is challenged is the differential treatment in the decision-making process. What is absolutely essential is uniformity in the application of standards and procedures. The rationale for an adverse promotion or retention decision must be performance related, such as unwillingness to accept responsibility for key administrative tasks or negative peer evaluations.

Although most discrimination suits are filed under Title VII of the Civil Rights Act, some are brought under the due process clause of the Fifth Amendment and a few under the equal protection clause of the Fourteenth Amendment. Suits filed on constitutional grounds impose on the complainant the heavy burden of establishing "intent to discriminate," which is not required under Title VII. In the latter case, only the results of a challenged promotion or retention decision need to be shown (Seldin, 1984). Thus, if an institution promotes a disproportionate number of male administrators and has no intent to discriminate against their female counterparts, a complainant would sue under Title VII and not on constitutional grounds. "Intent to discriminate" is obviously much more difficult to prove than discrimination inferred from "results."

To overcome a charge of race, sex, or ethnic discrimination, the institution must demonstrate that its evaluation measurements meet acceptable validity levels and that discrimination played no part in the promotion or retention decision. In general, the courts are reluctant to overrule administrative decisions but will intervene when the institution acts arbitrarily or capriciously.

Title VII requires that rating forms and other evaluation procedures bear a valid relationship to job performance. Blanket application of an evaluation instrument may fail to take into account that administrative assignments and specializations run a wide gamut. So, some formal analysis of the administrator's job must precede the development of a relevant evaluation system. It is a prerequisite to validate an instrument for the appraisal of performance.

Uniform Guidelines of Employee Selection Procedures. The Equal Employment Opportunity Commission (EEOC) is the enforcement arm of Title VII. In conjunction with the Civil Service Commission, the Department of Labor, and the Department of Justice, it has published a series of guidelines to help administrators perform their job of selecting and evaluating personnel within the law. Since these uniform guidelines were written jointly by the federal agencies charged with the enforcement of equal employment opportunity laws, they should be studiously followed in academia, if for no other reason than that the courts look to the guidelines as a reference for their legal decisions.

The guidelines allow a wide range of approaches to the appraisal of job performance, including interviews, work samples, and supervisory ratings. But the guidelines insist that whatever the approach, it must focus on important work behavior and be uncontaminated by prejudice in regard to race, sex, or ethnic background. Validation of the approach (or approaches) is mandated by the guidelines only when it adversely affects a race, sex, or ethnic group. It is prudent, therefore, to gather compelling evidence to validate the approach before implementing it (Seldin, 1984).

Important facts about what constitutes discrimination—and what may cause trouble for the institution—are readily available by telephone. The EEOC has installed a nationwide toll-free number (800-USA-EEOC or 872-3362) to answer questions about federal laws on discrimination based on age, handicap, race, religion, or sex.

Assessment Criteria and the Law

Colleges and universities continue to be vested with substantial discretion in evaluating administrative performance. A decade ago, Bickel and Brechner (1978) identified a developing legal trend that encouraged institutions to develop and disseminate to administrators the criteria, standards, and procedures governing evaluation. That trend continues. Over the years, many colleges and universities have developed public statements on the criteria and procedures governing administrative evaluation. It is readily acknowledged that these criteria are necessarily broad in scope and partly subjective, since the appraisal of performance requires the exercise of professional judgment.

As long as performance-related criteria are applied equitably and uniformly, the exercise of judgment, even though it may have been somewhat subjective, has been upheld by the courts. Generally, the college or university is required to demonstrate only that the evaluation was strictly performance related, that it contained no element of race, sex, ethnic, or other illegal bias, and that it was not arbitrary.

The courts generally do not scrutinize the particular methods or criteria employed by institutions in their evaluations, provided that they are clearly job related. And the courts generally are very reluctant to substitute judicial judgments for academic ones in such areas as sources of information, kinds of ratings, and relative weights given to the criteria. In fact, the courts generally have shied away from analyzing substantive methodology unless the charge of arbitrary or capricious decision making is leveled.

However, although the courts are generally not interested in disputes over methods and criteria, they exhibit great interest in three other kinds of disputes over the judging of administrative performance: (1) when the evaluation criteria are clearly spelled out in a legal contract between the administrator and the institution and are disregarded in practice, (2) when the evaluation criteria are so broad as to lack specificity or are not job related, and (3) when a discrimination complaint is filed against an academic institution under federal and/or state statutes (Seldin, 1984). Beckham (1986) finds that judicial review of personnel decisions should be expected when they appear arbitrary or capricious, lack supporting evidence, or deny the individual's legal rights.

All things considered, evaluation terms should be reduced to writing, either in standard format or in memorandum form. In addition, an appropriate supervisor should sit down and discuss the evaluation results with the administrator, provide thoughtful counsel on correcting deficiencies, and make notes on the meeting. As Bickel and Brechner (1978) point out, this procedure permits the administrator to erase the deficiencies and perform more effectively. Should the deficiencies persist, the ground has been laid for negative personnel action, and the likelihood that the negative action will end up in court is minimized.

Court Decisions on Administrative Evaluations

The curious truth of the matter is that the law has recognized few principles that can guide the academic administrator. However, from the limited case law available, some general legal notions can be identified and some conclusions can be drawn. The conclusions may not fit every situation, but they so closely parallel certain administrative practices that they deserve discussion.

Administrators should bear in mind that legal decisions

by judges are based on a set of facts and that each set of facts may contain different, even contrary, elements. Additional light is shed on the legal aspects of administrative evaluation each time a legal decision is made. Thus, administrators should proceed with caution in trying to grasp the significance of a particular decision for academic institutions. As Tucker (1984, p. 240) advises, administrators should "look to state statute, regulatory standards, institutional policy, and, where appropriate, collective bargaining agreements in order to clarify the legal obligations unique to each state jurisdiction. [In addition, relevant] legal standards vary depending on institutional type."

1. Liability of university and board in race discrimination suit—*Greenwood* v. *Ross* [778 F. 2d 448 (United States Court of Appeals, Eighth Circuit, 1985)]

Greenwood, a black male, was employed as an administrator at the University of Arkansas, Little Rock. When his supervisor was promoted, Greenwood applied for the vacated job. Rejected, Greenwood filed a race discrimination charge with the EEOC. Subsequently, he received a right-to-sue letter and brought suit in federal court, alleging violations of the Civil Rights Act. The university argued that its chancellor and board of trustees should be dismissed as parties to the suit. The district court dismissed Greenwood's claim, but the court of appeals found in his favor. The court of appeals held that the university and its board of trustees were suable for alleged race discrimination, where the cause of action was based on Title VII of the Civil Rights Act, as amended in 1972 (Bickel, 1986).

2. Evaluation of administrative staff—*Cripe* v. *Board of Regents* [358 So. 2d 244 (First District Court of Appeals, Florida, 1978)]

Cripe was employed as an administrator at the University of Florida. His immediate supervisor, Fox, was required under state rules to evaluate Cripe's work. As a result of an unsatisfactory evaluation, Cripe was terminated. He sued Fox and the board of regents, alleging that statements in the evaluation were defamatory.

The issue is: Is a defamatory statement in a performance evaluation required by the state absolutely privileged? The court held that it is. To hold otherwise, it reasoned, would defeat the purpose of the state rule requiring evaluation. Supervisors would hesitate to be candid in appraising performance out of fear of being sued for defamation (Bickel, 1978).

In the Cripe case the defamatory statement was made by the immediate supervisor. Question: Can a *peer* or *subordinate* be held liable for a defamatory statement in an evaluation? Black (1987) states that written or oral statements causing harm (that is, injuring a person in the exercise of a profession) are grounds for suit. However, *truth is an absolute defense to any such action.* The law protects the expression of one's legitimate opinions. Further, says Black, the courts today lean toward forcing complainants to prove that the words they find offensive are *not* true. This is an important shift in the burden of proof that makes it easier for the evaluator to defend the evaluation.

Performance evaluations have traditionally been protected by common law in the belief that public policy is best served by candor in such evaluations. Recent court decisions have continued this protection by ruling that there is no liability for evaluation statements unless the maker knew at the time that they were false or acted in reckless disregard of the truth in making them [*Colson* v. *Steig* (89 Illinois, 2d 205, 433 N.E. 2d 246) and *Belliveau* v. *Rerick* (504 A. 2d 1360)].

3. Evaluation of department chairperson—*Zink* v. *Lane Community College District* [578 P. 2d 471 (Court of Appeals of Oregon, 1978)]

Zink was appointed chair of the mathematics department of the community college. His written contract stated, in part, that before consideration for reappointment after a three-year term, he must undergo a comprehensive performance evaluation and, further, must do so prior to the termination date of the contract.

The college rules and regulations called for the department to designate one person other than the chair to administer the evaluation of the chair. Zink evidently failed to arrange for, and complete, the evaluation and received notice that he would not be reappointed as chair. He brought suit, the trial court found in favor of the college, and he appealed. The court interpreted the college rule to mean that the chair is responsible not only for the designation of the person to conduct the evaluation but also by implication for the completion of the evaluation as a precondition to reappointment. The court held that the complainant had not satisfied this responsibility and so had no contractual claim to reappointment (Bickel, 1978).

4. Reduction of salary after resigning as department chair—*Franken v. Arizona Board of Regents* [714 P. 2d 1308 (Court of Appeals of Arizona, 1985)]

Franken was recruited to the University of Arizona as a tenured professor and chair of the Department of Optical Sciences. He was a full-time administrator, as department chair, from 1975 to the 1984–85 academic year when he voluntarily resigned his administrative position to engage in full-time teaching. His resignation resulted in a salary decrease. Franken sued the university for breach of contract, wage discrimination, and denial of a property right (his salary). Question: Can the university decrease the salary of a tenured professor who voluntarily resigns as department chair to return to full-time teaching? Yes, said the court. Because Franken was tenured as a teacher, not as an administrator, his appointment as department chair was "at will." That meant he was not entitled to the higher rate of pay simply because he had previously received it.

5. Meetings to discuss evaluations of university president—*Missoulian v. Board of Regents of Higher Education* [675 P. 2d 962 (Supreme Court of Missouri, 1984)]

As part of its policy for university presidents, the board of regents assured confidentiality to all interviewees participating in performance evaluations of presidents. The *Missoulian*, an incorporated newspaper, formally requested admission to evaluation sessions between the board and certain presidents, as well as access to all evaluation documents. The requests were based on the state's Open Meetings Act and the "right to know" provision of the state constitution.

In court, the board argued that the evaluation procedure included frank discussions of the president's strengths and weaknesses, problem areas, rumors and accusations, and matters of family and personal health. The board insisted that such comprehensive discussions required confidentiality. Were the discussions to become public, the candor and integrity of the evaluations would be compromised.

The *Missoulian* argued that in matters of public interest the public's right to know outweighed considerations of privacy. When the district court granted summary judgments in favor of the board, the newspaper appealed to the Missouri Supreme Court.

The key issues: First, do university presidents have a reasonable expectation of privacy? Second, does that right outweigh the public's right to know?

The state supreme court found in favor of the board of regents on both questions. The court held that the expectation of confidentiality in the presidential evaluation was reasonable. It also held that the sensitive nature of the presidency suggests a sound reason to expect confidentiality in the evaluation process. In addition, the court noted that both the state constitution and the Open Meetings Act provide for closure of meetings and records when the demands for individual privacy exceed the merits of public disclosure. Such was the case here. The value of confidentiality was shown by, among other things: (1) the need to secure opinions from a wide range of persons who would not be candid except in confidence; and (2) the benefit to the public of effective, candid evaluations of its university presidents (Bickel, 1984).

What should you do when you think your university is going to be sued? Just as soon as an institution suspects that it may be sued, it should move promptly to protect itself by obtaining legal counsel. Underestimating the seriousness of a lawsuit is poor preparation for defending the institution.

When possible, rely on in-house counsel. The advantages are several: (1) in-house counsel is intimately familiar with the institution; (2) it is more likely that its advice will be readily available and timely; and (3) the cost will be less than for outside counsel.

However, in-house counsel may be inappropriate to defend all cases, especially those involving specialized areas, so outside attorneys may be needed. In selecting outside counsel, Black (1986b) suggests that the college or university consider the following questions:

- What is the attorney's reputation in this field?
- How many similar cases has the attorney handled? How many have been won?
- Is the willingness of the attorney to settle consistent with that of the institution?
- Does the attorney have sufficient time to devote to the case?
- Are backup attorneys and staff competent?
- What types of fee arrangements are offered?
- Is the attorney sympathetic to the institution's position?
- Does the attorney have any indirect contacts that could help resolve the case?

Alternatives to Litigation

Defense against a lawsuit is time consuming and costly. Not only may countless hours and dollars be expended in defense, but lawsuits also tend to have indirect, negative effects on the institution's operations, policies, reputation, and morale. Thus, institutions frequently offer to settle out of court. What are the alternatives to litigation? Black (1986b) reports two: negotiation and arbitration.

Negotiation. In conflict resolution, direct negotiation between the two parties may lead to a fair, acceptable arrangement. Differing, even hostile, opinions may be reconciled and underlying problems resolved before the two parties harden their positions in court. It helps considerably to maintain an informal environment in which the disputants can air their grievances and concerns in a spirit of earnest understanding. Should this fail, the attorneys representing the two sides can meet in a last-ditch effort to resolve the issues outside of court.

Arbitration. This approach employs a third party to settle the dispute. Both sides must agree on the choice of arbitrator, who generally has expertise in the disputed area, and agree to accept the arbitrator's decision as binding. The arbitrator may bring out points overlooked by the two sides, find areas for agreement, and come up with solutions reasonably acceptable to everybody. A ready source for all kinds of arbitrators is the American Arbitration Association.

The Association of Governing Boards of Universities and Colleges has circulated a proposal among leading higher education associations to establish a national center to help settle campus disputes before they reach the courts. Should sufficient support be forthcoming from these associations, reports Heller (1986), the Association of Governing Boards will seek foundation support for the project. The purpose of the project would be to identify successful campus-based procedures for averting litigation. In addition, it would assemble a cadre of conciliators to respond to campus requests for assistance in settling internal disputes. The conciliators would be academics, and their judgments would not necessarily be binding. Early reaction to the proposal has generally been favorable, but at this writing the governing boards have not yet sought foundation funds.

Due Process

When colleges and universities review their administrative evaluation practices they should pay close attention to due process. Constitutional due process means following certain principles, such as providing an administrator with proper notice of the reasons for the institution's action and an opportunity for a hearing on disputed issues of fact. Due process procedures are built-in safeguards against arbitrary or capricious action.

The application of due process to administrative evaluations is more than desirable; it is perceived as the administrator's right (Seldin, 1984). In two landmark cases, *Board of Regents* v. *Roth* [408 U.S. 564 (1972)] and *Perry* v. *Sindermann* [408 U.S. 593 (1972)], the United States Supreme Court established that administrators and faculty members in public institutions have a right to a fair hearing whenever a personnel decision deprives them of a "property interest" or "liberty interest" under the Fourteenth Amendment's due process clause. The "property" and "liberty" terminology is derived from the wording of the Fourteenth Amendment itself, which says that states shall not "deprive any person of life, liberty, or property, without due process of law."

Today, these Fourteenth Amendment guarantees are being applied by the courts not only to public institutions but increasingly to private institutions. Because almost all private colleges and universities receive some state or federal funding, they are open to additional court scrutiny.

In summary, colleges and universities must provide procedural safeguards to administrators whenever personnel decisions infringe on the administrator's property or liberty. For example, a decision to terminate an administrator in mid-contract must be accompanied by such procedural safeguards, since the decision clearly has an impact on property interests (Seldin, 1984).

Kaplin (1985) describes three basic situations in which courts will require a faculty nonrenewal decision to be attended by appropriate due process procedures. They are adapted here to administrators: First, the nonrenewal imposes a stigma or other disability that forecloses the administrator's freedom to take advantage of other employment opportunities. Second, the institution, in the course of nonrenewal, makes charges that could seriously damage the administrator's reputation, standing, or association in the community. Third, the existing rules, policies, or practices of the institution, or mutually explicit understandings between the administrator and the institution, support the administrator's claim of entitlement to continued employment.

An institution's procedures for making, and internally reviewing, personnel decisions should be in writing and made public. Such procedures can help the college or university avoid or rectify mistaken assessments, foster confidence in the institution, and encourage the resolution of nonrenewal or termination disputes in-house rather than in the courts. When such procedures do exist, the courts have been inclined to require administrators to exhaust all internal procedures before filing suit.

Seldin (1984, p. 28) points out that "if institutions follow their written procedures, in letter and in spirit, and provide compelling evidence to that effect, they are on firm legal ground. But when they depart from their own procedures, they become sitting ducks for suits and judicial condemnation."

For example, in *Sims* v. *Board of Trustees of North Florida Junior College* [444 So. 2d 1115 (District Court of Appeals of Florida, 1984)], the court found that the board of trustees failed to inform President Sims of his right to a hearing to discuss his contract's nonrenewal, and also the time constraints in filing his petition for a hearing. As a result, the court negated the commencement of the filing deadline and, in addition, reversed and remanded to the board for consideration of the petition.

The important point is that institutions must adhere to their own due process procedures. It is of no consequence whether the procedures were developed entirely by them, required by negotiated agreement, or extrapolated from state or federal law. What is important is that the procedures be followed explicitly.

In devising and reviewing evaluation procedures, colleges and universities should consider the procedural safeguards *before* making a personnel decision, not *after*. But what specific due process procedures should be followed before the institution decides not to renew an administrator's contract? Minimum due process safeguards would include: (1) written and publicized criteria for exemplary administrative performance; (2) a fair and evenhanded approach to administrative evaluation; (3) reasonable time to correct deficiencies prior to a second evaluation; (4) strict reliance on the rules of evidence in reaching personnel decisions; (5) a written statement of specific reasons for a negative decision; and (6) a well-defined appeals procedure.

There is no doubt that establishing evaluation procedures to provide due process requires considerable time and effort. But once such procedures are in place, disputes are more likely to be resolved by internal dialogue and conciliation than by the lengthy and costly adversarial process of the courts (Seldin, 1983). With very few exceptions, colleges and universities wish to be fair in appraising administrative performance. By building due process into the evaluation procedures, they help to guarantee that fairness. But due process demands more than lip service. It must be incorporated into the evaluation procedures and scrupulously adhered to in letter and spirit in practice. Strict adherence to the requirements of due process will go a long way toward assuring administrators that their performance has been evaluated in a careful, objective way and that decisions about them will be fair ones.

Checklist for Administrative Evaluation Programs

The following suggested checklist was developed from the EEOC guidelines, the current literature on legal aspects of administrator evaluation, and a review of recent court cases:

1. The results of a job analysis must be used in developing the content of the administrator evaluation system.
2. All parts of the program must be job related and subject to empirical validation.
3. An affirmative action program must be established to minimize the possibility of adversely impacting members of minority groups.
4. The criteria and procedures in the evaluation program must be provided in writing and in detail to all administrators.
5. The criteria and procedures must be scrupulously adhered to in letter and spirit.
6. Administrators must have current and accurate knowledge about the rights and responsibilities of institutions and individuals with regard to administrative evaluation.
7. Specific, written instructions must be given to all individuals who will be performing appraisals.
8. The individuals who evaluate performance must maintain sufficient contact with administrators and have frequent opportunities to observe their performance to be able to evaluate them accurately.
9. Evaluation forms must be written in clear and concise language.

10. Administrator ratings must not be based on vague and subjective factors.
11. Training in the use of evaluation instruments must be provided for the individuals who will evaluate performance.
12. Evaluations must be conducted and scored under formal, standardized conditions.
13. Considerable care must be taken—through measurement development, training, and ongoing review—to eliminate bias in regard to race, color, sex, religion, and national origin.
14. Multiple evaluation sources must be employed, and each source must be employed independently.
15. Self-appraisals must not be used for promotion or retention decisions.
16. Evaluations must be conducted in their entirety before personnel decisions are reached.
17. Hearsay evidence is impermissible in personnel decisions.
18. Administrators must be evaluated in accordance with established performance standards and the actual work assigned.
19. Administrators must be given timely and complete feedback on the results of their appraisals.
20. They must have the opportunity to respond in writing as to the relevance, accuracy, and completeness of their evaluations.
21. Personnel decisions must not be discriminatory in intent, application, or results.
22. Efforts to resolve personnel problems should be documented, the basis for the institution's authority to act should be articulated, and any action should be related to the valid objectives or statement of purposes adopted by the college or university.
23. Administrators who are given negative decisions must be given specific and valid reasons in writing.
24. Due process must be built into the evaluation procedures; that is, they must conform to the basic principles of evidence, allow the administrator to participate in the common effort to reach an accurate appraisal, and attempt to guard against undue subjectivity.

25. A formal appeals system must be part of the evaluation program.
26. Institutions must obtain maximum available insurance as protection against administrative liability in the event of a suit.
27. Legal counsel employed by colleges and universities must have current and accurate knowledge both of legal issues in academic management and of affirmative action and EEOC guidelines.
28. Colleges and universities must encourage a smooth working relationship between affirmative action officers and legal advisers.
29. Legitimate, nondiscriminatory reasons must be the actual basis for each employment decision.
30. Standards or criteria to guide personnel decisions should be subject to written limitations—in the contract between an administrator and the institution—if they are not intended to be legally binding.
31. Legal counsel must keep both institutions and their administrators informed of their current rights and responsibilities in evaluating performance.
32. The administrator evaluation program must not only contain no bias but also give no appearance of containing bias.

There is no ironclad guarantee, of course, that colleges and universities following the above suggested guidelines will not be sued. But the possibility of being sued and losing the case in court will be sharply reduced.

Institutions must bear in mind that the courts are first and foremost the guardians of process. They are far less likely to become involved in disputes concerning the substance of standards and criteria than in disputes over procedures for enforcing standards and criteria. It is the procedural defect in the policy of a college or university that often creates the basis for litigation.

Preventive Law

Traditionally, the role of the legal profession in colleges and universities has been one of resolving problems created by campus policies, programs, and decisions. It has focused on actual challenges to institutional practices and on affirmative legal steps by the institution to protect its interests when they are threatened. The goal has been to resolve the specific legal problem at hand. This is known as *treatment law,* and it is indispensable to the functioning of colleges and universities today (Black, 1986a).

But recently, increased attention has been paid to a different type of campus legal need. It is known as *preventive law* and is designed to maintain legal health. It focuses on initiatives that the institution can take before actual legal disputes arise. Preventive law systems are designed to identify legal problems and solutions for colleges and universities through continuing review of case law and administrative rules and regulations, as well as continuing review of federal and state constitutions. In preventive law, says Kaplin (1985, p. 32), "Counsel identifies the legal consequences of proposed actions; pinpoints the range of alternatives for avoiding problems and the legal risk of each alternative; sensitizes administrators to legal issues and the importance of recognizing them early; and determines the impact of new or proposed laws and regulations, and new court decisions, on institutional operations."

Although preventive law has not been a general practice in the past, as the presence of the law on campus has increased, the acceptance of preventive law has grown significantly. Today, preventive law is as indispensable as treatment law and provides a more constructive and positive basis from which to conduct institutional legal affairs.

The following steps are suggested by Kaplin (1985) for institutions seeking to implement a preventive law system:

1. Review the institution's current organizational arrangement for obtaining legal counsel. Determine whether changes—for example, from outside firm to inside counsel—are appropriate.

2. Develop a teamwork relationship between senior administrators and legal counsel. Both must be involved in legal issues and cooperate with each other on a regular basis for preventive law to work effectively. It is the job of the attorney to resolve doubts about the interpretation of statutes, regulations,

and court decisions and to suggest legal options on their relative effectiveness in achieving the institution's goals. It is the job of the senior administrator to have current and accurate knowledge about the theory and practice of academic administration and to develop legal policy options and determine their relative effectiveness in achieving institutional goals.

3. Conduct legal audits at regular intervals. Conducted by the attorney–senior administrator team, the audit is a means of determining the legal "health" of the college or university. Every office and function should be audited periodically to determine whether it is in compliance with the full range of legal constraints to which it is subject.

4. Develop an early-warning system that will alert counsel and senior administrators to potential legal problems. The system should be based on a list of situations that the institution is likely to encounter *and* that are likely to create some significant legal risk. For example, such a list might include situations where the system used to evaluate the performance of academic deans is being revised, a committee is drafting or modifying an affirmative action plan, or a college is seeking to terminate the contract of the academic dean. Under the early-warning system, these situations—and others like them—would trigger a consultative process between senior administrators and counsel aimed at resolving legal problems before they start.

5. Engage in continuing legal planning. Using the data obtained through legal audits, early-warning systems, and other means, it is possible to assess risks and to avoid problems or resolve them before they become too threatening. Legal planning establishes the process by which the college or university determines the degree of risk exposure it is willing to assume in particular situations and avoids or resolves legal risks it is unwilling to assume. Teamwork between senior administrator and attorney is a critical ingredient in legal planning. So is sensitivity to the authority structure because decisions about legal planning must be made at the appropriate level of administrative authority.

6. Establish an internal grievance mechanism to resolve as many disputes as possible within the campus community. What techniques can be used to resolve disputes? They include

informal consultation, mediation or arbitration, and hearings before panels drawn from the academic community. True, some disputes are not amenable to internal solution. But many others can be resolved through grievance mechanisms, thus forestalling the complainant's resort to the courts or other external bodies.

To some extent, the need for colleges and universities to practice preventive law has led an increasing number of institutions to establish in-house legal counsel. Black (1986a) says that in 1961 only eight institutions reported having such positions. By 1984, however, a survey by the National Association of College and University Attorneys found that 47 percent of the 268 institutions surveyed had full-time resident legal counsel. Among the respondents with annual budgets exceeding $50 million, 70 percent had in-house counsels (Fields, 1985).

Conclusion

Where colleges and universities have published criteria and standards that guide administrator evaluations, the courts are reluctant to invade the process of academic governance. But the courts show no such reluctance in three other kinds of disputes: first, when there is a dispute over the application of criteria; second, when the evaluation criteria lack specificity and/ or are not job related; and third, when a complaint of discrimination is filed against an institution.

Nothing is more damaging to an institution's defense in a legal action than evidence of duplicity, deceit, or discrimination. Regrettably, such evidence has been uncovered at more than a few colleges and universities, even though chicanery, scheming, and half-truths clearly have no place in an institution of higher learning.

Certain practices have been found to be associated with the successful legal defense of administrator evaluation systems. They include the following dicta: (1) use specific, objective, job-related standards (avoid the use of trait-oriented criteria); (2) establish a meaningful affirmative action program; (3) give written instructions to all individuals who will evaluate performance; (4) ensure that individuals who rate performance have had sufficient contact with the persons being evaluated to rate them accurately; (5) provide training for those who evaluate performance; (6) provide administrators with prompt feedback on the results of their appraisals; (7) provide for meaningful due process.

Development and implementation of legally sound administrator evaluation programs will not eliminate all legal disputes. But the number of such disputes will be severely reduced. When an evaluation system is characterized by good faith and fair dealing, both the institution and its administrators are the beneficiaries. Equally important, the evaluation system inclines toward the improvement and reward of administrative performance, where it properly belongs.

The next two chapters will address the development of administrative performance.

⊁ 6 ⊀

Strategies for Developing and Improving Administrative Performance

The contemporary academic administrator deals with a bewildering array of tasks and issues. The administrator is expected to perform as a master manager of financial, physical, and human resources, and to display the skill of a surgeon, the wisdom of a Solomon, and the strategy of a field general. Very few administrators are aware of *these* requirements when they first assume their posts.

The core problem, of course, is that most administrators have not received training in the skills demanded of them. They lack the knowledge, the preparation, and the requisites for effective administration. A doctorate in physics in no way prepares the individual to be the chairperson of the physics department—nor to be the dean of the college. This is not to suggest that the untrained administrator necessarily is a mediocre administrator but that he or she is forced to acquire skills mostly through trial and error (Gaff, 1975).

In the words of a former president of the University of Cincinnati: "I am more and more impressed with the almost total lack of any rational career plan for academic administrators. Most of us got into this work adventitiously, and most of us do what we have observed others do when they were in these roles

145

or emulate, incorrectly, some other shadowy figures of the past, fantasies of Harvard Business School products, General Patton, creatures of fiction or movies, or some atavisms of leadership and authority which never were" (Bennis, 1973, p. 397).

Roach (1976) points out that the typical chair is a subject matter specialist within a discipline, who has been selected because of his or her scholarly achievements and not because of any impressive display of management skills. In fact, many academic administrators firmly believe that the most essential qualification for their positions is solid experience as a faculty member. This belief is embodied in job advertisements for presidents, vice-presidents, and deans in the *Chronicle of Higher Education.* In the advertisements, an earned doctorate is almost always required, but training in administration, if mentioned at all, is described simply as a desirable asset.

Millett (1978) divides the administration of a college or university into two parts. One part is "support," and it includes library facilities, student services, plant operation, and development. Administrators in these areas are likely to have had professional education, ongoing professional training, and a predictable career ladder of experience on which they have climbed to their present positions. The other part of administration is "academic," and it includes instruction, research, and public services. Administrators in these areas, typically the president, vice-president for academic affairs or provost, college dean, and department chairperson, have had precious little professional training for their positions and confront a precarious career ladder.

The need to improve the training of academic administrators has long been recognized. In 1923, the first in-service training sessions for college presidents, deans, and personnel officers were given at the University of Chicago's Institute for Administrative Officers in Higher Education. More recently, in 1962, the Phillips Foundation Program of Internships in Academic Administration was initiated. The American Council on Education's Academic Administration Internship Program became operative in 1964, and the Harvard University Institute for Educational Management in 1970. Calls for professional development of administrators have appeared regularly in the literature (see Bauer, 1955; Bolman, 1964; Henderson, 1970; Mauer, 1976; Eble, 1978; Tucker, 1984).

Today, many academic administrators manage to acquire skills before and after assuming administrative positions, but the overwhelming majority simply have to piece together their experience without benefit of in-service or other training. Nevertheless, there are signs that the situation may be changing. As a specialized field, higher education has been developing in the past twenty-five years, and administration has been one of the beneficiaries. More colleges and universities are offering on-campus seminars and workshops for their academic administrators. More professional development opportunities, both regional and national, are available. In short, administrative development is finally getting more of the attention it deserves (Seldin, 1987).

What has kindled the change? A few key reasons include the growth of management accountability, the need to keep pace with new technologies, the recognition of the inherent relationship between evaluation and development, the spillover effect of faculty development programs, the greater emphasis on self-actualization as a goal for professionals, the better understanding of the stages of adult development, and the success of prestigious programs for administrative development at Carnegie Mellon University and Harvard University.

Professional Development of Administrators

Just about every college and university administrator is in need, in one or more areas, of professional and personal development and job improvement (Edwards and Pruyne, 1976; Miller, 1985; Seldin, 1987). It may be the need to update personnel policies, legal issues, trustee relationships, or planning and budgeting, or it may be the need to hone personal skills and operating strategies in connection with leadership, communications, time and stress management, and delegation. It may be the need for personal renewal.

Gaff (1975) offers some key principles of faculty development that are adaptable to administrator development:

1. Regardless of age, experience, or effectiveness, all academic administrators are capable of development.
2. When offered the opportunity to improve performance, large numbers of administrators will accept the offer.
3. Programs seeking to improve performance stand a better chance if they include attitudes, values, skills, and sensitivities than if they focus on narrow concerns (for example, budget-preparation techniques).
4. All colleges and universities harbor some administrators with special expertise. These administrators should be identified and persuaded to share their expertise with their colleagues.
5. Since administrators are members of social groups, it is often necessary to work with an entire administrative unit (for example, the office of the dean, including the academic dean, associate and assistant deans, executive secretaries, clerical support people, and receptionists) to improve the administrative climate.

The Role of Experience. How important is experience in the professional development of administrators? Nichols and Sharp (1985) report that nearly 70 percent of the deans and directors in a survey acknowledged that experience on their own campus turned out to be the most important influence on their professional development. Sagaria and Krotseng (1986) report that the academic deans in their study called program planning and implementation their most important managerial skill and that past experience had yielded valuable knowledge in this area.

But what does it mean to have experience? How does one describe the inner nature of experience? Everyone claims to recognize experience, but coming up with a serviceable definition of it is like tilting at windmills. Campbell (1987) suggests three important components of experience. First, it is necessary to learn the business, which frequently means learning the relevant vocabulary. Second, one must make contacts or become part of an academic network. *Experienced* people tend to know a lot of other people who can make things happen, while *inexperienced* people are limited to a small covey of acquaintances. Simply knowing hordes of people is not enough, however. Loyalty, respect, trust, and shared values are needed ingredients. Third, it is imperative to learn the rules of the game—the ethics, values, norms, and expectations at the college or university.

Is the pattern of developmental experiences the same in all institutions? Lombardo (1986) says no. Each institution has its own unique developmental profile. The events experienced may be roughly similar, but their frequency and intensity differ among institutions. Certainly the developmental pattern is shaped by the attitudes and values expressed and/or implied by top-level administrators. Their methods for dealing with people, communicating with them, and rewarding or punishing them suggest to other administrators how to do things and draw the dividing line between what is acceptable and what is not.

Do highly effective administrators learn the same lessons from experience as ineffectual administrators? No, says Lombardo. The high performers learn lessons from important job assignments (directing an institution-wide self-study, for example) that stimulate their development as administrators. The low performers either fail to learn any lessons or learn them in some obscure way. The reason? Perhaps the low performers simply do not comprehend their experience. If so, their comprehension needs jogging and assistance from other administrators.

Firsthand experience, especially over the long run, has its partisans as a way to acquire administrative knowledge. But trial-and-error learning comes with a high price tag for both the administrator and the institution. The institution should not have to bear the burden of an administrator's ineptness and inefficiencies while he or she learns how to become a good manager. Fisher (1977) points out that learning the art and science of administration is a continuing process, achieved most effectively by a combination of day-to-day experience and administrator development activities. These activities may include release time for study and travel (including visits to other campuses), institution-sponsored seminars and workshops, internships, informal professional reading, and participation in programs offered regionally and nationally.

Resistance to Administrative Development. Curiously, the academic community, which believes in and supports education for a wide variety of professional occupations—law, business, and medicine, to name only a few—has been slow to accept the idea of professional education for college and university administrators. Resistance to the notion of professional development has somewhat eroded in recent years, but it still solidly entrenched in many institutions of higher education.

Some academic administrators who are troubled by their inwardly acknowledged insufficiencies feel uneasy and even threatened by anything or anyone trying to evaluate their performance. Under threat, they may react by avoiding or attacking the threatening situation or person. They try to defuse the situation or in some way render it impotent and may even attempt to undermine the academic reputation of the person who is perceived as a threat.

Much of this resistance arises from conditions in higher education regarded as unfairly burdensome. Some of these conditions are:

1. The expectation that an administrator can improve his or her performance without a supportive institutional environment.
2. The misuse of evaluation data gathered for improvement purposes and applied to salary and promotion decisions.
3. Adding an additional activity, such as attending a weeklong, off-campus seminar, to an already overworked administrator's schedule.
4. Failure of the institution's reward system to support administrator development activities.
5. Failure of graduate programs to prepare doctoral students to be administrators as well as researchers and teachers.

Add to these inadequacies the common human tendency to resist any change, the distrust that some administrators have for each other, and their tendency to resist getting involved in instructional activity, and you have entrenched opposition.

Tucker (1984) adds a few more reasons why administrator development activities are stonewalled. The administrator's personal goals may not be consistent with the institution's goals. The administrator may shrug off the idea of pursuing professional growth and recognize no need for developmental activities. A different reason is offered by Eble (1978). He suggests that resistance to formal training for college and university administrators may stem from the adult's resistance to any learning that intrudes upon areas of the psyche close to the centers of personality and character.

Resistance to development also arises from myths and misconceptions surrounding attempts to beef up administrative performance. Like other popular myths and misconceptions, they are difficult to dislodge. Crow and others (1976) cite a number of myths in connection with faculty development that are also readily adaptable to administrative development:

1. Good administrators are born, not made.
2. The effective administrator needs no help; the ineffective one is beyond help.
3. Since administration is an art, not a science, it cannot be learned.
4. Only the less effective administrator has room to improve.
5. The whole administrative development movement is a ploy to lower academic standards.
6. Academic administration is an impenetrable process and defies analysis.
7. An evaluation of administrative performance is an invasion of academic freedom.
8. Only good administrators should be hired, and institutions should then get out of their way.
9. How the administrator functions is not the institution's business.

It is not a purpose of this book to attempt to dispel these myths and misconceptions. There exists a rich literature addressed to these and related issues. But how should they be dealt with on campus?

One proven method is to invite a nationally renowned scholar or specialist in professional growth. Since much of the hard-core resistance to administrative development feeds on myths and misconceptions, the scholar or specialist should address each of these in clear, forthright language. The reasons why, case studies, the benefits to the administrators and the institutions should be presented. Questions can then be answered and resistance slowly overcome. However, participation in these seminars should be voluntary.

Administrative Behaviors and Attributes

In academia, as in the business world, there is a full range of administrative behaviors and attributes—good, bad, and in-between. The literature, as well as practical experience, provides many examples of behaviors and attributes to be cultivated and others to be avoided. The good ones tend to enhance the institution and its staff, the bad ones to damage both. Are they readily distinguishable? Yes.

Unfortunate Behaviors and Attributes. Horn (1986) identifies some unfortunate characteristics and kinds of behavior common in administrators whose performance fails to match their early promise. They include an irresistible urge to place others on the defensive; an unchecked drive for status; an abrasive, aggressive personality (sometimes mistaken as the hallmark of a "natural leader" and a good administrator); an inability to manage the special complexities of a large institution (or a small one); an inability to create a cohesive institution, to face up to performance problems, or to delegate appropriately.

McCall and Lombardo (1983) add to the list an insensitivity to other people, a failure to do *what* the administration promised to do and *when* it would be done, and a failure to apprise others in advance of changes of mind or direction.

Klumph (1986) suggests that ineffectual administrators often miss warning signals of future organizational difficulties. Among these signals: (1) fewer and fewer administrators and faculty asking meaningful questions; (2) complacency, a feeling of comfort with things as they are; (3) less and less risk taking by middle- and upper-level administrators; (4) deteriorating lines of internal communication; (5) a lack of interest in how things are done in other colleges and universities; (6) a parrot response to the fresh ideas of others—"we tried that a couple of years ago and it didn't work"; and (7) a campus on which clone-like thinking flourishes.

Stevens (1982) finds that less effective administrators tend to be shallow, defensive, rigid, guarded, and worried. They possess a limited understanding of the position they hold, including its power and limitations. They are neither articulate nor persuasive, cannot deal with uncertainty, and are inconsiderate of their associates.

Another undesirable attribute is the constitutional inability of the less effective administrator to say no to patently unreasonable requests to take on extra tasks. The administrator accepts the tasks not because they will add satisfaction and meaning to his job but because he is too docile to exercise his own judgment. In effect, others determine what the administrator does and who he or she is (Many, 1986).

Actually, if a single administrator possessed all these negative characteristics, any professional development of him or her would best be written off. The poor soul would simply be beyond redemption and should seek a job outside higher education. But the vast majority of academic administrators, who probably exhibit at least a few of these behaviors, are prime candidates for professional development. They have no place to go but up.

Desirable Behaviors and Attributes. What are desirable behaviors and attributes common to effective campus administrators? Gilley, Fulmer, and Reithlingshoffer (1986) list these: an orientation to people, vision, awareness of opportunity, visibility, and a practical approach to problem solving. Douglas (1984) comes up with (1) adjusting and adapting to change, (2) knowing the students as much as individual and institutional circumstances permit, (3) encouraging faculty and students and supporting their efforts to excel, (4) recognizing and acknowledging a job well done, (5) remembering that people make an institution function, (6) becoming personally involved throughout the institution instead of serving as a figurehead, and (7) allowing faculty members enough freedom to do their jobs yet being ready to step in to meet a crisis or a unique opportunity.

Seldin (1987) represents the following behaviors and attributes as essential: (1) a responsiveness to service, (2) a willing-ness to lead, (3) an ability to deal with detail without being swal-lowed up by it, (4) an effective use of time, (5) an ability to keep goals always in mind, (6) a capacity to marshal fresh energy, (7) an understanding of both the psychic and the material needs of people, and (8) an embracing of high ethical and moral standards.

At times, an institutional crisis arises that sorely tempts the administrator to issue technically correct but misleading in-formation. But it is always best to hew to the truth. Tampering with the truth may haunt the administrator in the future be-cause a lack of integrity in the upper echelons of administra-tion will sooner or later manifest itself in the lower levels of the institution.

Regardless of rank, each administrator must contend with the problem of getting things done. Eble (1978) offers nine axioms as aids in getting work done efficiently and effectively:

1. The way to big accomplishments is through painstaking at-tention to small details.
2. Sorting out what there is to do is a first step toward getting it done.
3. Dealing with people is more taxing and time consuming than dealing with things.
4. Doing the things you do not want to do first can save the day for things you do with enthusiasm and satisfaction.
5. A job assigned may not be a job well done.
6. Learning to write and speak simple, serviceable English and to handle simple business machines can be powerful aids to getting things done.
7. Developing a strong office staff begins with dignifying the work that needs to be done.
8. There is never enough time. The able administrator makes the available time fit.
9. You will always fall behind; you will never catch up.

A fundamental difference between the more effective and the less effective administrator is how they handle the power of their position. Walker (1979) and Beidler (1984) are persuaded that effective administrators have the capacity to separate themselves from their offices and wear the status and privileges of position lightly. This does not mean that they distance themselves from the academic community. As Rosovsky (1987, p. 40) states: "Distance from peers results in the inability to hear constructive gossip. That gap also undermines administrative authority, which should be based on the principle of PRIMUS INTER PARES rather than on rank and commands. More serious, perhaps, is the resulting difficulty of getting unpopular decisions accepted. This will happen more easily if 'we are all in the same boat' is not a farce."

McCall (1978b) says that administrators must understand that enormous power carries with it enormous responsibility for its use. The responsibility is not only moral, because few abusers of power ultimately escape the consequences of their acts. Green (1986, pp. 18–19) cautions that when a lone administrator, even acting under stress, uses the power of office to move an institution single-handedly, the institution will suffer damage: "When the crisis has passed, the leader will inevitably have to pay attention to the frightened and demoralized faculty who were not fully part of the rapid change process. . . . To ignore the traditions of faculty input and the need for self-determination threatens the ability of an institution to continue to plan, adapt, and move forward as a body. . . . Few can lead long without the consent of the governed."

The National Center for Higher Education Management Systems ("Organizational Effectiveness . . . ," 1984) has also developed a list of desirable behaviors and attributes. The center argues that administrators should (1) use images, stories, and symbols to reinforce an institution's purpose and goals; (2) nurture the patronage of important constituencies; (3) distinguish between the institution's character and direction and political pressure; (4) provide the kind of environment in which mistakes can be made in the interest of learning; (5) guarantee the institution's traditional mission prior to implementing change; (6) respect the institution's culture; (7) communicate trust, openness, and loyalty to staff members, particularly under difficult or threatening conditions; and (8) maintain integrity and personal character.

Are all the desirable behaviors and attributes cited in this chapter learnable? They are. But they must be cultivated through selected professional development activities.

Desirable Features of a Development Program. Ryan (1976) says that professional development programs should be geared to well-defined needs to be successful. The needs of one administrator may differ somewhat from the needs of the next administrator. Administrators are not cut from the same mold. It is a patent waste and may even be counterproductive to try the same professional development activities on all administrators.

In general, performance will improve when administrators (1) are alerted to alternate ways of behaving, (2) accept that change is desirable, (3) believe that change is feasible, (4) receive supportive feedback on their behavior, (5) are emotionally engaged in the developmental process, and (6) are complimented and rewarded for their improvement. Nothing helps consolidate professional development better than recognition by the institution's reward structure.

To succeed, an administrative development program should include certain salient features. The following list is compiled from the work of Lindquist (1978), Bedsole (1979), Miller (1985), and Seldin (1987):

1. The program should rest on the axiom that perfect administrative behavior is as unattainable as it is undefinable.
2. The program should reflect the institution's needs, values, and culture.
3. Administrators should feel, with justification, a sense of ownership of the program.
4. The environment for development should be supportive and in no way threatening.
5. Administrators should support each other in their development activities.
6. The program should address both the performance of administrators and job satisfaction.
7. Top-level administrators should boost the program with vocal public support.
8. The institution should support the program with funds for professional development both on and off campus.

9. Plans for individual development should be consistent with institutional objectives.
10. Progress in development should be recognized.
11. The program should have a personal development component to go hand in hand with and facilitate professional growth.
12. In addition to developing skills, the program should provide training in role-relevant behavior, guided practice, and feedback to refine the behavior.
13. The program should develop competency in interpersonal communication, group process, and conflict management.
14. The program should promote administrative team building.
15. Incentives should be offered by institutions to motivate administrators to continue to practice the desired behaviors.

Strategies for Administrative Development

A number of optional strategies are available to strengthen administrative performance. Selection of the appropriate strategy depends on such factors as (1) the rank of the administrator, (2) the specific areas needing improvement, (3) the financial support available for professional development, (4) the beliefs of campus administrators concerning professional development, (5) time constraints, and (6) the administrator's motivation to strengthen performance.

Evaluation. This is frequently the entry point for professional development and is commonly used to improve performance. It rests on the assumption that improvement becomes possible when the administrator is confronted with evaluative data showing strengths and weaknesses—data that the administrator accepts as fair and accurate. Performance evaluation can thus serve as a springboard for performance improvement. But actual improvement depends on three factors: whether the evaluation turns up judgments new to the administrator, whether the administrator is motivated to improve, and whether the administrator knows how to improve.

Evaluation is more likely to have a salutary effect if its results are discussed with the administrator by a sympathetic colleague. The administrator needs reassurance that the disclosed problems are neither unusual nor insurmountable. The colleague can then offer advice on how to improve.

Discussion. Unlike the evaluation approach, this strategy is rarely perceived as threatening by administrators. It is based on the assumption that an exploratory discussion among professional administrators will yield insights and keener understanding of administrative styles and even a more definitive educational philosophy. A variety of administrative issues and problems are discussed. In the course of discussion, the participants clarify their own assumptions about academic management and investigate alternative modes of performing tasks.

Sometimes the assembled administrators are asked to reflect on specific questions, such as:

- Why did you decide to become an academic administrator?
- What do you enjoy most about administration? Least?
- If you were not an administrator, what would you like to be?
- If this were your last term as an administrator, what would you do differently?
- As an administrator, what is your greatest strength? Your greatest weakness?
- What is your greatest administrative accomplishment? Your greatest failure?

In the course of group discussions, each participant also learns that other administrators share his or her uncertainties and self-doubts. What emerges from the discussion are more self-aware and self-confident administrators.

I can attest to the value of discussion from personal experience. Some years ago I was associate dean of the College of Business, one of four associate deans at Fordham University (New York). Although we served in different colleges, our duties and responsibilities mostly coincided. We decided to meet monthly to discuss nuts-and-bolts issues of common concern. Though informal, the meetings were structured and lasted about seventy-five minutes. We exchanged how-do-you-handle-it answers to campus problems. We bared our thoughts in seventy-five candid minutes. For the four participants, the meetings were an extraordinary development experience.

Specific Administrative Skills. This strategy is based on the belief that improvement in performance results from training administrators in new skills. The training sessions include short- and long-term courses and workshops aimed at introducing basic management principles, innovative methods, and organizational development issues to the administrators. Virtually all programs are process oriented. The goals may vary, but almost all courses and workshops, whether on campus, regional, or national, move beyond discussion to provide hands-on experience for participants. In most cases the emphasis is on doing rather than on talking, on the practical rather than on the general.

Programs run from a day or two to several weeks, with the shorter programs tending to be more thematic in nature and to address a single problem or issue. They telescope relevant learning experiences. One-day workshops confined to faculty evaluation, for example, have been offered on campus by numerous institutions, including Sullivan County Community College (New York), St. Olaf College (Minnesota), Gallaudet University (Washington, D.C.), Mount Saint Vincent College (New York), West Virginia University, Appalachian State University (North Carolina), Columbus Technical Institute (Ohio), and Texas A & M University.

Some programs are more constituency oriented, paying special attention to a particular administrator's role as it relates to basic concerns and administrative problem solving. For example, the American Assembly of Collegiate Schools of Business offers in alternate years a four-day New Deans Seminar, an introductory series for new academic deans. The seminar topics include planning for change, internal and external resource development, automating the dean's office, faculty evaluation, accreditation, executive development, internationalizing the business school curriculum, legal issues, and opportunities for school-industry cooperation.

Other programs cut across the administrative hierarchy. The American Council on Education, for example, offers a two-day leadership development program designed for academic vice-presidents, provosts, deans, and division and department chairs. Among the topics are policy and procedural issues, legal issues, techniques for reviewing academic and nonacademic programs, and governance structures that can have an impact on program review decisions.

Reward System. If administrators are denied reward after improving their skills, they will tend to lose interest in the development program. That is readily predictable. While there will always be some administrators who find sufficient motivation in enhanced self-esteem and job satisfaction, most administrators look to rewards in terms of salary increases, greater authority, and promotion.

The reward system provides other avenues for recognition of improved performance. Some institutions offer nominal grants to administrators who want to experiment with new administrative techniques. Others offer released time or sabbaticals to be used for study or travel. Still others offer so-called growth contracts as a means of improving performance.

Growth Contracts. This approach eliminates two problems that cause some development programs to fail. The two problems are anemic incentives for professional change and lackluster supervisor support. What is a growth contract? It is a detailed written plan of future progress, prepared by the administrator and approved by the supervisor, that contains a description of the administrator's present duties and responsibilities, a self-assessment, a succinct enumeration of performance goals and a timetable for their achievement, a learning and development scheme linked to each goal, a discussion of the means of measuring each goal's achievement, and an enumeration of budgetary and other needed support.

Seldin (1980a, p. 82) states that individualizing the program achieves two important objectives: "First, it enables the administrator to reflect on his or her professional strengths and weaknesses, which can later be translated into feasible goals for the year. As the administrator grows, the institution is the beneficiary. Second, the program achieves evidence by year's end of which goals were achieved and which professional activities fell short."

A climate of acceptance is indispensable if the growth contract is to be embraced by the administrator. One way to gain this acceptance is to field-test the contract on a handful of senior administrators. The fact that they willingly expose in writing their previously hidden administrative weaknesses will not be lost on other administrators. These field tests not only provide administrators with useful experience but also permit modification of the contract, should that be advisable.

A related technique is role definition. Zion (1977) states that role definition provides the administrator with (1) a clear understanding of his or her role in the institution, (2) an awareness of the means to perform that role, (3) a recognition of the skills and abilities needed to implement the means, and (4) an opportunity to acquire and enhance those skills and abilities. The process begins with a written rationale of the administrator's position, a definition of his role, and a description of his job. An inventory of skills and abilities needed to fulfill the role is then drawn up. Both the administrator and immediate supervisor decide on the skills and abilities that need acquiring or strengthening. That becomes the basis for a three-year growth plan.

Career Development. As a strategy, career development requires more than conceptual learning. It requires the development of specific competencies, such as planning and problem solving, conflict management, and interpersonal communication (Boyer and Grasha, 1978). For behavioral change to lead to performance improvement, the development program must go beyond skill training. It must focus on diagnosis of role performance and training in role-relevant behavior.

Some colleges and universities establish programs to aid administrators in planning their careers and undertaking revitalizing activities. McMillen (1986a) describes the joint program sponsored by the agricultural colleges of the universities of Minnesota and Nebraska. Supported by a grant from the federal government's Fund for the Improvement of Postsecondary Education, the program provides about $1,400 to each administrator (or faculty member) to develop growth plans that spell out personal and professional career goals. Each participant (1) takes part in an off-campus retreat in which he reflects on his career; (2) completes the Myers-Briggs Type Indicator, a psychological test indicating basic personality traits and career preferences;

and (3) learns to evaluate reasons for the importance of their career achievements. For some participants there is no immediate payoff. But for others, the program has led to career changes or has at least recharged the individuals professionally.

The University of North Carolina, Greensboro, has designed a pilot program on career leadership and development for female administrators. The program, which includes two half-day seminars and a one-and-a-half-day workshop, covers career stratagems, goal setting, negotiating and managerial skills, building administrative credentials, networking, long-range planning, fiscal management, and fund raising. Barriers faced by female administrators are discussed in detail. A special feature of the program is the career-development sessions in which participants receive one-to-one counseling.

What makes a career development program successful? Leibowitz, Farren, and Kaye (1985) report that the most effective programs are

- tailored to the institution's culture
- designed for their long-term impact but build for short-term payoffs as progress is indicated
- structured with multiple approaches to meet individual preferences, schedules, and styles
- assured of clear and visible support from top-level administrators
- aided in their design and management by advisory groups
- publicizing their accomplishments along the way, not just at the end
- started small, perhaps as pilot projects targeting specific needs or groups

Organizational Development (OD). This strategy assumes that individual performance improvement must be supported by group policies and procedures if it is to endure. Richardson (1975) is persuaded that OD is needed for individual development. The overall goal of OD is to enhance teamwork within the entire college or university. Emphasized are the interpersonal aspects of administration. For example, if administrators in different areas are often at odds, OD helps them resolve differences and encourages cooperation. OD relies on group discussion, techniques for constructive confrontation, and other methods to terminate inter- or intragroup conflicts. OD focuses on whole institutions or their subunits and seeks to improve overall functioning by applying the principles of group process and change.

Internal or external consultants (or facilitators) work with top-level administrators to develop the OD approaches most likely to succeed. The consultants serve primarily as catalysts for change and help group members acquire the sensitivities, knowledge, and skills needed to improve the effectiveness of the institution.

What are the steps in the OD process?

1. The consultant meets with top-level administrators to determine the nature of the institution's problems and to develop appropriate approaches to them.
2. Research is conducted. In attitude surveys and interviews, the level and nature of job satisfaction, supervisor-subordinate relations, group policies and procedures, morale, and other interpersonal relations are determined. Also probed are the actions needed to improve group functioning.
3. Work groups are assigned to review the collected data, to mediate among themselves areas of disagreement, and to establish priorities for change.
4. The group develops recommendations for change as well as plans detailing who is responsible for taking the action and when it should be taken.
5. The consultant encourages groups to analyze how they work together so that they recognize the value of open communication and trust as prerequisites for better group functioning.
6. The results of the OD effort are evaluated and additional programs are developed as needed (Davis and Newstrom, 1985).

Deans, presidents, department chairs, and others interested in the finer details of the OD process might consider participating in the Leadership for Educational Change program sponsored by the NTL Institute. The six-day residential program is offered each summer in Bethel, Maine. The program is designed to assist participants to develop (1) their educational philosophy and learning theory; (2) their knowledge of how to apply OD, planned change, and professional development theory and practice; (3) their insight into their own leadership style and interactive skills; (4) their ability to develop and participate in leadership teams; and (5) their responsiveness to racial, gender, and other human differences.

Reading. A widely used approach to picking up new ideas and enhancing administrative performance is simply by reading (Scott, 1976). A chronic time shortage, along with a distaste for group programs, has caused some academic administrators to rely on reading for their professional development.

For the administrator with just a foot of vacant bookshelf and very little time, the following books are particularly recommended: *The Department Chair* (Booth, 1982); *Academic Strategy—The Management Revolution in American Higher Education* (Keller, 1983); *Managing the Academic Department* (Bennett, 1983); *The Law of Higher Education* (Kaplin, 1985); *Higher Learning* (Bok, 1986); *The Academic Dean: Dove, Dragon, and Diplomat* (Tucker and Bryan, 1987).

Also recommended are these articles: "Applied Research on Leadership in Community Colleges" (Hall and Alfred, 1985); "Leadership and Learning: The College President as Intuitive Scientist" (Birnbaum, 1986); "Presidential Opinions on Today's Key Issues" (Budig, 1986); and "The Ups and Downs of Deaning" (Rosovsky, 1987).

Lastly, administrators seeking an overview of what is happening in higher education would do well to become members of the American Association for Higher Education and to subscribe to the *Chronicle of Higher Education*. Both are located in Washington, D.C.

Heuristics. This approach to developing administrative performance assumes that the primary objective of any change should be to provide administrators with the skills to identify and solve their problems without continued dependence on others. The method is to interrupt ineffectual problem-solving strategies and substitute more effective ones. This may involve, for example, uncovering previously withheld information and/or maximizing internal commitment to policy decisions. Heuristics are readily learned devices for breaking old action patterns and applying new, more effective ones.

Heller (1982) states that a heuristic approach has three components: a *flag* that indicates when it should be used; a *recognition* of what is happening in the situation at a correct level; and a concise prescription for what to *say* and how to *act* toward another person. Consider the following heuristic sequence designed by Heller (p. 93) to deal with an apparently unresolvable conflict:

> Flag: When win-lose arguments develop.
> Recognition: Participants need some alternative method for resolving disagreements. Specifying the information that would settle the issue is one such method.
> Say: I do not see how we can settle this disagreement with the information available. If you agree that we cannot solve the problem without more information, what kind of information could we gather that you would accept as disconfirming your interpretations? What could we do to get that information?

In summary, there are various types of administrative development activities. There is no unique formula for strengthening performance. The approach must be situational. The "right" approach today may be inappropriate in five years. Whichever approach is used, however, must be grounded in the current situation and be consistent with the convictions of the administrator.

Implementing an Administrative Development Program

How a development program is put into place in a college or university is just as critical as *what* that program is. Installing the program is a process of organizational intervention. Following are some general guidelines and strategy suggestions to help implement a successful program.

Lindquist (1978) suggests a nine-step approach: (1) assess individual and organizational needs; (2) focus on problem solving; (3) emphasize peer teaching and support; (4) clarify administrative goals, roles, competencies, and rewards; (5) conduct a series of related seminars using a development facilitator to maintain momentum; (6) organize a mentor system; (7) organize task groups to execute development activities; (8) close development meetings with action plans; and (9) use growth contracts.

The Stordahl (1981) incremental plan for faculty development has been adapted here for administrative development. It includes the following steps: (1) provide the rationale for the development program, (2) assign responsibility and authority for planning, (3) involve the administrators in planning, (4) provide sufficient flexibility to meet the different needs of administrators, (5) balance institutional and individual needs, (6) keep participation voluntary, (7) reward participation, (8) consider alternative approaches to be used in the program, (9) mix internal and external resources, (10) publicize the program, (11) evaluate the results, and (12) provide adequate funding.

The approaches suggested by Lindquist and Stordahl are models of common sense. Their experience and the experience of others suggest the wisdom of proceeding slowly, attentively, and openly and laying the groundwork for the program's successive steps.

It is of vital importance to think big but start small. A well-planned development activity for a small group of administrators is more likely to achieve success than a general effort for a large group, which may suit no one in particular. Expectations will be preserved at a realistic level if a low-key, low-profile approach is used (Tucker, 1984). A small group of satisfied volunteers is the best advertisement for more ambitious activities.

Finally, just as student and faculty performance can be improved, so can that of academic administrators. Development activities have clearly established their worth in the acquisition and strengthening of behaviors, attributes, sensitivities, and skills. No one would make light of the hurdles confronting administrators intent on improvement. Progress may be slow. The effort may possibly fail. But the stakes for higher education are high. It is imperative to try.

President John F. Kennedy was fond of telling a story about the French Marshall Louis Lyautey. When the marshall announced that he wished to plant a tree, his gardener responded that the tree would not reach full growth for more than a hundred years. "In that case," Lyautey replied, "we have no time to lose. We must start to plant this afternoon."

The next chapter will examine in-house and off-campus approaches to developing administrative performance.

✳ 7 ✳

Providing Opportunities for Professional Development On and Off Campus

Learning the science and art of academic administration is a life-long process. After an individual has absorbed the principles of administration, learning how to implement these principles occupies the rest of his or her working life. Just as the attorney, accountant, doctor, dentist, and other professionals practice their crafts, so does the administrator practice administration. Recognition of the administrator's professionalism is relatively recent in academia. Aiding the professionalism of the department chair, dean, provost, or academic vice-president are rapidly multiplying programs, both in house and off campus. They are all designed to teach administrative skills and techniques and to imbue academic administrators with the spirit of managerial professionalism.

In-House Development Activities

Numerous colleges and universities are assessing their administrative needs and implementing their professional development programs. On-campus programs have several important advantages. They simplify the transfer of learning, provide more frequent and continuing training, and are less expensive than off-campus ones. Even more important perhaps, they address the immediate and pressing needs of administrators at a particular institution.

The growth of in-service programs in recent years has been nothing short of phenomenal. Fisher (1977) reports that a 1976 survey by the American Council on Education found less than 300 colleges and universities offering some kind of in-service administrative development program. By 1987 more than 900 institutions were offering such programs (Seldin, 1987). Activities now range from workshops and seminars to retreats and internships. Topics covered include MBO, administrative stress and time management, budget preparation, long-range planning, the process of change, faculty development, and evaluation.

Higher Education Management Institute (HEMI). It is often difficult for individuals to modify their behavior patterns without corresponding changes in the institution. One resolution of the problem is to employ developmental strategies throughout the institution. This approach is recommended by HEMI. Located in Coconut Grove, Florida, HEMI was founded in 1976 for the purpose of designing an institution-wide organizational development plan for higher education. For its program HEMI adapted the organizational effectiveness model of Rensis Likert to higher education. The comprehensive Likert model includes the assessment of management tasks, processes, activities, and skills (Booth, 1982). The HEMI program, which focuses on the work group, is based on the assumption that administrative development must come from within the institution. So the institute develops training modules for institutions and offers on-site instruction to their staff members on how to lead the training sessions (Brookshire and Tally, 1978).

The HEMI program is composed of five phases: introduction, needs assessment, action planning, implementation, and evaluation. In the introductory phase, the institution learns the details of the program. The needs assessment involves the gathering of data about the administrative approach at the institution. Action planning reviews the data with an eye for locating areas needing improvement; a plan is then formulated to improve each area. Implementation involves development programs for work groups and individual administrators. Finally, the evaluation phase measures the satisfaction level of the participants and the individual and institutional performance.

Seminars, Workshops, and Institutes. Many colleges and universities have introduced professional development programs to train presidents, provosts, deans, and department chairs in areas such as financial planning, strategic decision making, quality controls, communication, data collection and management, computer modeling, and environmental scanning (Keller, 1983). Not only do these programs produce new skills, but they also raise awareness of sensitive issues among academic leaders.

A caution is in order. There is wide diversity among colleges and universities. There is also wide diversity among the administrators in a single institution, in their experiences and administrative talent. It is critical, therefore, that the following programs not be accepted without adapting them to meet local needs and traditions. They are guides, not blueprints.

As for topics, which are addressed by institutions in their in-house development programs? And which institutions offer the programs?

Department Chairs. The University of Utah has a program that brings department chairs, novice and experienced, together to discuss such matters as (1) recruiting and retention (finding and keeping good people); (2) the department and its publics (student affairs, public relations); (3) budget (how to procure and save money); and (4) deadwood (what to do with faculty members who are no longer productive). The program was developed at minimal cost and by the participants.

Since department chairs are the front-line administrators for teaching and learning, Virginia Commonwealth University devised an attitudinal workshop: each chair is interviewed to determine his or her attitude toward chairing the department, leadership ideas, teaching and learning beliefs, and professional aspirations. A series of small-group sessions and exercises follow to help chairs specify their assumptions, clarify their values, and enhance their leadership styles. Finally, there are consultation with individual chairs and follow-up assistance to any department member requesting it.

One-day workshops have been offered to department chairs by Loyola University (Illinois) on time self-management, Augsburg College (Minnesota) on administrative leadership, Pace University (New York) on preparing the departmental budget, Montana State University, Sullivan Community College (New York), and the University of Delaware on evaluating and developing faculty performance.

Fairleigh Dickinson University (New Jersey) has developed a low-cost model for training department chairs in leadership skills and giving them practice in solving actual problems. The pilot project was conducted in the College of Science and Engineering, and Lucas (1986) reports that the content of the workshop was developed following a needs assessment. Meeting weekly for three hours over ten weeks, the department chairs (eight plus the dean and associate deans) discussed: (1) the role and responsibility of the chair, (2) leadership and communication, (3) motivating faculty members to assume greater responsibility in departmental affairs, (4) resolving conflict through problem solving, (5) performance counseling, (6) team leadership and effective group behavior, (7) departmental decision making, (8) stimulating departmental change, (9) managing departmental conflict, and (10) goal setting, evaluation of training, and follow-up program. Each session included minilectures, case studies, role playing, and simulation exercises based on actual problems generated by the chairs. Using actual problems served to validate the program for the participants, since solutions to their problems were suggested.

The University of Tennessee has devised a multifaceted program to develop the skills of chairs. Blom (1985) reports that the program includes three elements. First comes skill training. Each campus of the university has constructed a series of short training programs dealing with university systems. The purpose is to build skills and understanding in such areas as personnel benefits, fiscal policy and procedure, and the human resource information system. The programs, presented by top administrators, generally run one-half day and are held on campus.

The next step is management training. The primary vehicle for this training is the Model-NETICS Program, which strives to sharpen skills by giving a working understanding of management principles. The program makes heavy use of mnemonic devices, involves forty hours of classroom work, and gets participants to focus on learning the models that represent key management principles. The models, functioning as guides to thought and action, address such subjects as compensation, motivation, planning, and decision making. The third and final element of the program is the Institute for Leadership Effectiveness. The institute conducts an off-campus program in two parts, each lasting four days and separated by six months. Part one includes a history of the university, personal style, campus culture, group-development cycles, political and economic pressures confronting the university, and leadership in higher education. Part two includes conflict management, leadership effectiveness, organizational issues, and ethics. A full day is devoted to simulating a working organization to demonstrate the behaviors common in the university. The institute, funded centrally, has a training staff of ten, which is assisted by resource speakers from within and from outside the university.

Deans, Provosts, and Presidents. Top administrators at Miami-Dade Community College (Florida) attended an ongoing seminar for two years to sharpen skills in such areas as MBO, goal setting, designing programs, and evaluating goal achievement. The group participated in training exercises designed to create a climate of trust in which feelings and thoughts can be shared candidly and participants can learn from each other. The result is better interpersonal relationships and more effective team building, as participants learn management concepts and techniques (Gaff, 1975).

Wichita State University (Kansas) has produced a continuing program to promote leadership abilities and techniques to deal with flat or declining economic conditions. Outside lecturers, workshops, retreats, and seminars increase proficiency of deans and vice-presidents in planning, decision making, and alternative futures modeling (Buchtel, 1980).

When Warren Bennis was its president, the top twenty-five administrators at the University of Cincinnati attended an ongoing seminar on management and organizational development. The seminar, which consisted of visiting speakers, readings from their books, and discussion, was part of an overall effort to analyze the role of the professional manager for the institution's administrative staff.

Perhaps the largest in-house training program is operated by the University of Texas. There, the Institute of Higher Education Management runs workshops from two to five days for deans, chairs, vice-presidents, and presidents of the fourteen campuses of the university. The subjects include financial forecasting, academic planning, faculty evaluation and development, decision making, budgeting and allocations, assessment of programs, and schools and institutions (Keller, 1983).

Southwest Texas State University offers an in-house, three-year development program for deans. Some of the subjects offered are management skills and practices, innovative methods and materials, trends and pressures, and sharing common concerns. The subjects are broken down into workshops and seminars that cover (1) being a new dean; (2) on-the-job training; (3) academic planning; (4) time management; (5) budget; (6) MBO; (7) advanced MBO; (8) the art of delegation; (9) leadership and motivation; (10) secretarial/staff development; (11) communication skills; (12) stress management; (13) financial management; (14) law, courts, and the academic administrator. Each workshop or seminar is a self-contained unit. Some are offered just once (for example, time management) and others (for example, academic planning) are updated annually.

A sampling of other institutions with programs includes the University of Minnesota, Duluth, on planning and giving effective presentations; the University of Western Ontario on managerial skills; Ryerson Polytechnic Institute (Canada) on leadership styles and stress; the Pennsylvania State University on evaluating and developing faculty.

The North Carolina Community College Presidents' Leadership Institute also merits mention. The institute was formed to develop presidents of community colleges in the state in the area of leadership renewal. Campbell (1986) reports that the institute was designed for the following goals: (1) to plan strategically to utilize appropriate forms of new technology, (2) to improve institutional management and decision making, (3) to strengthen the partnership between trustees and president, (4) to enhance productivity and quality educational programs, (5) to update occupational programs for the emerging technologies, (6) to apply new resource development and marketing strategies, and (7) to evaluate the impact of the community college on learners and the community.

The institute was organized into seven three-day sessions at different host campuses throughout the state. Lectures and seminars were augmented by active group involvement through discussion and case studies. The format made it possible for the presidents to learn more about current research and practices and apply what they learned to their own campuses. Thirty-eight community college presidents participated in at least one institute session, and nearly twenty attended three or more.

Discipline-Based Training. Since 1963, the Association of Departments of English has sponsored summer seminars for department chairs on administrative and educational matters (Booth, 1982). The seminars balance discussions of pragmatic issues of departmental administration with discussions of new trends that might affect English departments. Small groups led by experienced chairs discuss day-to-day management issues.

The Teaching Resources Program of the American Sociological Association has developed a workshop for chairs to complement its program to improve undergraduate education. Similar workshops have been developed by the Association of Foreign Languages.

The Council of Graduate Departments of Psychology offers an annual workshop for new chairs designed to cushion the shock of becoming an academic manager. As described in *Academic Leader* ("Management Wisdom," 1986), some of the suggestions at the 1986 workshop were based on the work of Kimble (1979): (1) be aware that at least 25 percent of your day will be spent on things you did not expect to be working on that morning; (2) the chair can greatly enhance his or her position just by knowing what is going on in the institution; (3) it is important to know details—where the money comes from, where the students come from, who teaches what, when, and how your department compares with others in terms of numbers of students and faculty, office space, and budget; (4) ask for advice in making decisions; (5) keep good records; (6) be clear about goals and objectives; (7) delegate by setting up good faculty committees; and (8) groom a successor.

In-House Administrative Development on a Small Budget. When available funds and the needs for administrative development do not match, colleges and universities are likely to compute the cost of each proposed development program to be sure it will not unbalance the budget. This can be useful at the close of a problem-solving process after all options have been examined. But when inserted at the start, it often results in a truncated plan that pleases no one.

Are there no-cost or low-cost administrative development ideas available to institutions with skimpy budgets? There are. Fisher (1977) is convinced that strengthening administrative performance need not be an expensive process. By using local resources and a little ingenuity, a college or university can implement significant professional-growth activities. For example, informal staff seminars, interoffice mini-internships, and peer teaching and learning are recommended. These activities should focus not only on today's problems but also on the emerging concerns, trends, and opportunities of tomorrow.

Whitcomb (1986) describes a few no- and low-cost ideas for faculty and organizational development. They are adapted here for administrative development: First, when administrators attend conferences, encourage them to commit themselves in advance to a subsequent feedback session to share what they have learned with their colleagues. Second, allow a few days between semesters for seminars by administrators for administrators on topics of professional interest. Third, invite administrators who present papers at regional or national meetings to repeat their presentations for colleagues on campus. Fourth, team senior and novice administrators so that they can share practices and policies that work and discuss campus mores and resource support. Fifth, promote the circulation of articles and papers of professional interest. Sixth, ask administrators to present working papers for reaction by colleagues before submitting the papers for review. Seventh, ask faculty members from management and psychology to present so-called window workshops on the management of time, stress, and conflict. Ask other qualified faculty members to lead noonday exercise or meditation sessions. Finally, use quality circles to decrease costs and increase administrative efficiency.

Mentoring. As recorded by Homer in the *Odyssey*, Mentor was the servant of Odysseus entrusted with wide-ranging responsibilities in the care and training of Odysseus' son, Telemachus. The possibility that senior administrators can develop the skills and attitudes of less experienced administrators is receiving fresh attention in the business world. Kantor (1984) argues that companies anxious for excellence should encourage managers to be mentors to their employees. Kotter (1985) states that mentors, sponsors, coaches, and role models are positioned to be of special importance in the development of administrators, particularly early in their careers. Much impetus for the renewed attention given to mentoring comes from Japan, where *sempai-kohai* (senior-junior) relationships have been successful for years. Lee (1986) suggests that the college and university environment is even more conducive to mentoring than the more turbulent world of business.

A young academic administrator cannot will a relationship with a mentor. It must emerge from the touching of two lives. Raines (1986, p. 46) comments that a mentor relationship "must have the reciprocity of a good romance. The adulation of the younger must be received with a sheltering affection that, in time, ripens into mature respect between equals. Carried to full term, it is a bond more complex and subtle than that between father and son, a kinship cemented by choice rather than biology."

Mentoring relationships are quite distinct from other kinds of work relationships, and the functions of mentoring can be summarized in two broad categories. *Career functions* are those aspects of the relationship that accelerate "learning the ropes" and advancement in a college or university. Included here are activities such as enlisting public support for the mentored person's career, aiding him to gain exposure and visibility in the organization, coaching him in specific strategies, protecting him from negative influences, and steering challenging and constructive assignments toward him. *Psychosocial functions* are those aspects of the relationship that help produce competency, clarity of identity, and effectiveness in a professional role. The mentor's attitudes, values, and behavior are role models. The older administrator supports and encourages the younger colleague and helps him over personal hurdles that may interfere with work productivity.

The two colleagues are often friends who understand each other and enjoy each other's company (Kram, 1985). As a management professor from New York describes it: "We liked each other from the beginning, when I was interviewed for the job. When I came to the university we often had lunch together in the park. We talked about everything, the university, sports, politics, literature, our families, our hopes. We enjoyed spending time together."

Mentor roles can be filled by many persons. They may be persons within the institution or from outside it. They may be co-workers, higher-level administrators, spouses, friends. What is important is to develop a network of mutually supportive relationships in which a host of individuals provide a variety of mentoring functions.

One of the most compelling features of the relationship is that it feels so special. Daloz (1986) notes that the younger colleague feels uniquely "seen" by the mentor and that when the mentor is endowed with exceptional qualities or powers, the effect can be electrifying. As a provost from California describes her first encounter with her mentor: "I was awed by her. The woman was absolutely brilliant. Her vocabulary, command of the subject, self-confidence, and general demeanor were beyond anything I had ever witnessed. It was as if I were talking to God."

Is the relationship one-sided? Not at all. Not only does the mentor gain satisfaction in parceling out the benefits of long experience, but he or she also enjoys technical and psychological support from a very loyal younger person and is recognized by others as an effective developer of talent. Consider a comment by the president of a Minnesota college: "Spending twenty years in administration, as I have, gives me quite an array of valuable experiences. What better to do than share them with some bright, young people. I assure you, it is not simply a philanthropic gesture on my part. I get hard work and loyalty in return. And I know that the board of trustees has taken positive note of my mentoring."

It is necessary to underscore, however, that certain factors on a college or university campus can promote or interfere with mentoring. Similarly, individuals may be promoters or detractors of mentoring, depending on their attitudes. And some individuals may lack the interpersonal skills required to build supportive alliances. A few of the organizational and individual obstacles to effective mentoring include (1) an institutional reward system that fails to recognize the importance of human resource development; (2) the lack of performance-management systems, including systems for appraisal and career development; (3) diminished opportunities for older and younger administrators to interact; (4) an institutional culture that discourages mentoring and other relationships between administrators; (5) individual assumptions, attitudes, and skills incompatible with developing the relationships needed for mentoring (Kram, 1985).

External Opportunities for Administrator Development

Even a cursory examination of any issue of the *Chronicle of Higher Education* reveals the profusion of seminars, institutes, and workshops on administrator development offered monthly. The array of topics is formidable. Programs vary in sponsorship, scope, and audience. Some are sponsored by national or regional associations, some are commercial ventures, and some are sponsored by individual colleges or universities. The time range is from one day to more than three weeks. Some curricula are confined to the responsibilities of a particular set of administrators (presidents, for example), while others focus on a mixed group with overlapping responsibilities in one area (strategic planning, for example).

In addition to increasing their cognitive knowledge, participants gain from the exchange of ideas and experiences with other attendees, during class and out of class. There is also the opportunity to become part of a new network of professional colleagues. With regard to selecting one professional development program over others, there are obvious trade-offs. Given the ever-present budgetary and time constraints, a program must be selected with unusual care. It must address the administrator's most urgent needs and in the most meaningful way. Fisher (1979) offers some self-questions to guide the selection process:

1. Does the program speak directly to your needs and those of your institution?
2. Are the topics congruent with your interests?
3. Who are the speakers and program faculty? What are their qualifications?
4. What are the instructional methods? Will the participants be active learners or part of a passive audience?
5. Does the conference design allow a balance of activities and session options? Does the schedule allow out-of-class assimilation time and social interaction? Are some meals taken as a group?
6. Will the group be small enough to encourage interaction, camaraderie, and the building of long-term acquaintances, yet large enough to introduce a variety of stimulating ideas and experiences?
7. What types of administrative positions and institutions will be represented? Is there sufficient diversity for cross-fertilization of ideas yet sufficient commonality to make it possible to address matters affecting your own job or setting?
8. How accessible is the conference site? Is it isolated enough to keep the group together yet not so remote as to make it inconvenient and costly to reach?
9. Can you and your institution afford the program's time and cost?

10. Is there provision for the participants to evaluate the learn-
     ing experience at the program's conclusion or at a later
     point?

The factual questions raised by Fisher can be answered
by asking for additional information and descriptive materials
from the contact person or organization named in the advertisements. The judgment questions, however, can be answered only
by the prospective participant, who must get out a balance scale
to weigh the pros and cons.

Although the number of external development opportunities is quite impressive, they fall conveniently into five categories: short, thematic programs; longer, more comprehensive
programs; national or regional conferences; internships; and
Outward Bound training.

Short, Thematic Programs. These generally have an open-
admission policy, last one to five days, and cost several hundred
dollars. Not always but quite often they are thematic in nature.
One of the programs offered in 1987 was "Higher Education
Management Strategies" presented by the Division of Continuing Education, University of Virginia. This was a four-day workshop on various management techniques and their implications
for higher education. Topics under discussion included conflict
resolution, leadership, decision making, budget planning, staff
development, and legal parameters.

"Shaping Today's Community College Mission for Tomorrow's Expectations" was a two-and-one-half-day institute
sponsored by the University of Michigan. It covered such topics
as trends shaping community colleges in the 1990s; adapting to
the environment; the mandate for change; public policy, opinion, and expectations; managing change in the organization; degree and nondegree programs; external relations; and staff development and utilization.

"Chairing the Academic Department" was presented by
the American Council on Education in Washington, D.C. Among
the topics in the three-day program were the role of the chairperson, departmental program review, performance counseling,
progressive discipline, faculty evaluation and development, legal

liability of the department chair, recruitment and affirmative action, working with nonacademic personnel, bringing about change, dealing with conflict, and maintaining faculty morale.

"Leadership Development" was offered by the Center for Creative Leadership in Greensboro, North Carolina. A five-day program, it is offered approximately twenty-five times each year. Topics include assessment, the creative leadership process, decision making, situational leadership, leadership style indicators, utilizing group resources, innovative problem solving, principles of feedback, and setting and achieving goals. A special feature of the program is peer and staff feedback to the participants on their leadership behaviors.

"Increasing College Income" was presented by Memphis State University (Tennessee). A three-day workshop for college presidents, it covered improving fund solicitation, improving marketing and student recruitment, improving student retention, and making public relations effective.

"How to Make a Difference in Washington" was designed for new business school deans by the American Assembly of Collegiate Schools of Business. The four-day program covered the congressional policy-making process, business schools' prospective influence on that process, state government politics and higher education, corporate political activities and trends, and issues affecting management education.

"Legal Issues in Academic Management" was offered by the Higher Education Resource Center in Denver, Colorado. The three-day seminar, fashioned for senior academic administrators, addressed academic employment relationships, faculty handbooks and appointment contracts, student catalogues and handbooks, the contract of enrollment, nondiscrimination and constitutional rights, and sexual harassment.

"Adult Learners in Higher Education" was sponsored by Central Michigan University. Topics in the two-day program were the impact of adults on higher education, types of programs appropriate for them, how to improve delivery of course content, and partnerships of higher education and business.

Longer, More Comprehensive Programs. Admission to these programs is by application and the competition is stiff.

The programs last several weeks and cost from $2,600 to $3,600. Rather than focus on a central theme, they are more comprehensive in content. The following programs were presented in 1987 and are repeated annually:

The Harvard University Management Development Program (MDP) is a two-week residential program for administrators who are likely to hold such titles as chair, director, dean, or associate dean. The fee is $2,750. In 1987, the MDP curriculum, which is based to a large degree on case studies, included the following topics: (1) human resource management, (2) faculty personnel policy and administration, (3) financial management, (4) law and higher education, (5) decision making, (6) small-group leadership, (7) leadership and organization, (8) cultural diversity in higher education, (9) issues in the structure and governance of colleges and universities, and (10) the future of higher education.

The Summer Institute for Women in Higher Education Administration is a three-and-one-half-week program sponsored by Bryn Mawr College (Pennsylvania) and Higher Education Resource Services (HERS), located in Denver, Colorado. The fee for resident participation is $3,500; for nonresident participation (space permitting) it is $2,500. The program is designed to elevate the status of women in middle and senior levels of higher education administration, an area in which women have traditionally been underrepresented. The institute provides training in finance and budgeting, long-range planning, human relations skills, administrative uses of the computer, organizational management, and academic governance. Strategies are also presented for professional development with emphasis on leadership, management, and career planning. Thereafter, the institute provides a continuing supportive network of peers and mentors. The guest faculty, in residence for varying periods of time, lecture or conduct workshops in their special fields. They represent business, government, and a cross section—public and private—of small and large colleges and universities.

The Carnegie Mellon University College Management Program (CMP) is a three-week residential program for senior administrators, mostly deans and vice-presidents. The fee is $3,500, and the curriculum concentrates on strategic planning, leadership, academic services and faculty quality, shifts in funding from government and private sources, and environmental changes that impact on institutions. The program makes extensive use of case studies, in-class exercises, role playing, and other instructional techniques for involving participants and facilitating discussions. The teachers are particularly distinguished and include eleven persons who are currently vice-presidents, presidents, or chancellors. Additionally, there are ten nationally renowned speakers from education or business.

The CMP includes the following subjects: (1) designing your institution's future; (2) revitalizing your institution; (3) strategic planning; (4) marketing; (5) building an effective public relations program; (6) improving admissions; (7) managing personal staff; (8) computing; (9) improving fund raising; (10) financial aid allocations; (11) managing institutional change; (12) leadership; (13) evaluating teaching quality; (14) managing technology on campus; (15) working with deans and department heads; (16) politics of institutional change; (17) the future of higher education; (18) managing academic stress; (19) improving faculty performance; (20) budgeting and fiscal planning; (21) transitional leadership; (22) dealing with government leaders, agencies, and legislators; and (23) working with the board of trustees.

What are the benefits of the more comprehensive institutes and seminars? The main one, of course, is that the participants learn more about various subjects. But other benefits include the feedback that participants receive on their performance from colleagues in the program. The participants also have an opportunity to measure themselves against their peers from other institutions. Attendees may even gain a competitive edge when they seek higher administrative positions.

Regional or National Conferences. For some administrators, professional development comes from the formal and casual exchange of ideas and information at regional and national meetings.

Typical of the regional meeting is the Annual Regents' Conference on Higher Education sponsored by the Board of Regents of the State University and College System of Tennessee. Among the frequently discussed topics are strategic planning for excellence, characteristics of institutions that have good retention records, equity through excellence, institutional image and marketing strategies, university–private sector partnerships, accreditation issues, values, preparing students for the work world, and evaluating faculty performance.

At the national level, the National Conference on Higher Education, sponsored by the American Association for Higher Education, each year attracts about 2,000 participants, mostly administrators. The conference includes keynote addresses, plenary and concurrent paper presentations, evening receptions, newcomers' breakfast, business meetings, exhibits showcasing nearly forty major commercial and nonprofit enterprises that serve colleges and universities, research forums, action communities, program briefings, low-cost thematic workshops, special activities such as black caucus meetings, and position round tables for certain administrators.

Thus, for participants at the conference the problem is not finding a subject of interest, but selecting from so many attractions.

Internships. For those with administrative potential but not yet in top-level administrative positions, an internship program may be the answer. The internship experience enables an individual, under a mentor's guidance, to test his or her aptitude for and interest in administration. The intern is free to study, observe, and learn unencumbered by the responsibilities and constraints of a job. The combination of guided experience plus study is a particularly effective approach to professional development.

Stauffer (1978) points out that the internship also (1) provides an opportunity to evaluate the pros and cons of academic administration as a new career without requiring a firm commitment, (2) permits direct involvement in high-level academic policy making and managerial routine, (3) helps the institution identify and evaluate faculty members and junior staff who have demonstrated potential for becoming effective academic administrators, and (4) enables senior administrators to sponsor and develop the leadership of the future.

The American Association of Community and Junior Colleges inaugurated an internship program in 1986. Those professors or junior administrators selected as fellows spend between three months and one year at the association's Washington office, with a community college president and a state college official, either in a congressional internship or conducting individual research. Splitting the internship among several settings is encouraged.

Perhaps the best known national internship program is the American Council on Education (ACE) Fellows Program, which provides a year-long internship for thirty fellows annually. Working closely with presidents and senior administrators who serve as mentors, fellows observe and participate in all aspects of institutional administration. The Fellows Program has created a pool of highly trained leaders who have both in-depth administrative experience and a broad perspective on higher education.

Do most of those who participate in the program actually move into senior administrative positions? They do. Of 843 persons completing the program from its founding in 1966 through 1985, 101 individuals have become presidents, and 435 others have served as deans and vice-presidents. Moreover, in a survey of the fellows, 80 percent indicated that the program had been decisive in their choice of career paths.

Fellows serve as interns either on their home campus or at host campuses. What do fellows do on campus? Among other things they (1) attend all decision-making meetings, (2) serve as executive assistants to the chief executive and chief academic officer, (3) work on projects such as the revision of faculty handbooks and the development of early retirement policies, (4) write position papers and speeches, (5) use the fellows network to gather information about institutional practices on other campuses, and (6) write a fellowship paper.

Fellows work directly with at least two mentors who are top administrators on campus. They are the key teachers, since fellows learn by doing. The mentor helps fellows plan their year and monitors their progress. Mentors are encouraged to attend at least one of the three fellows' seminars. Conducted in September, January, and May or June, these five-day seminars expose the fellows to up-to-the-minute thinking on key issues in higher education. Seminar topics include budgeting and financial management; financial and academic planning; collective bargaining; faculty personnel issues; theories of management and leadership; legal issues; financial aid; curriculum planning, evaluation, and revision; future problems; federal policy (*ACE Fellows Program Information Brochure*, 1987–1988).

Though not strictly an internship, as defined above, international visitation schemes offer administrators comparable developmental experiences and an opportunity to view key managerial issues from a different perspective. As we approach the twenty-first century, we must recognize the greater economic interdependency among nations and the remarkable advances in communication technology. The concept of the global village has become a reality. Like it or not, international cooperation will probably be mandatory to solve complex managerial problems in higher education. Culbertson (1981) remarks that if administrators in higher education are to be adequately prepared for the next century, they must acquire a world perspective.

Murphy (1984) proposes an international visitation plan for college and university administrators. It would bring together colleagues from different socioeconomic environments to discuss administrative areas of common concern. A theme might be long-range planning. Structured learning experiences for the administrators would include guided visits to local institutions and government agencies, where discussion of managerial and administrative problems would be encouraged. Not unduly to disturb professional and personal lives, the intervisitation would be limited to three weeks. A few weeks later, Murphy suggests, the administrators from the host community would return the visit and avail themselves of similar learning experiences and opportunities for professional development.

Outward Bound Training. This approach to off-campus professional development is unique. It teaches administrators to reach for answers in the face of severe physical conditions, the belief being that the experience will help the administrators improve their effectiveness on campus. Outward Bound training has been more readily accepted in the business world than in academia. A number of corporate executives from Federal Express, Xerox Corporation, Martin Marietta, Coors, and AT&T have participated in the program. In academia, Wake Forest University (North Carolina) and Dartmouth College (New Hampshire) have offered the training to graduate business students. Carnegie Mellon University offers the training to business executives.

What is Outward Bound training? It involves logistical and skill-developing activities taught in wilderness areas to small groups by experienced instructors. It includes mountain climbing, white-water canoeing and rafting, sea kayaking, and cross-country skiing. The training is said to foster teamwork, creative problem solving, a willingness to take risks, and a tapping of latent energies (Rein, 1983). It is believed that administrators learn better by actually doing rather than by sitting in workshops or reading books. The training builds confidence and self-worth in the participants and a more sensitive awareness of, and confidence in, those with whom they work.

Outward Bound, which opened its training programs in 1962, offers an array of professional and career development courses that emphasize learning in four major areas: leadership, teamwork, risk taking, and professional renewal. For a four-to-nine-day period, the outdoors literally becomes a classroom. Participants scale high walls, climb mountain summits, and negotiate rapids. Experienced instructors are skilled in drawing analogies between each activity and the work world in debriefing sessions and lectures throughout the course. The cost ranges from $600 for a four-day program to $1,050 for a program of nine days. The programs, which are offered in Oregon, Colorado, Maine, North Carolina, and California, are, if nothing else, challenge oriented. As a chair from a California college remarked, "The instructors push your emotional, physical, and spiritual limits."

As might be expected, these training programs include some unusual incidents. Fowler (1984) reports that each member of one group was told to select a piece of paper and perform whatever task was written on it. One administrator read that she was to run one-half mile. Another administrator picked a paper that contained a *London Times* crossword puzzle without clues. Another found that he had "up" and "down" clues but no puzzle. The last two sat quietly, unable to perform their tasks, while the woman set off on the half-mile run.

The aim of the exercise was to point up the importance of cooperation and exchange of information. The two who were given parts of the puzzle later realized they could have completed the puzzle had they talked to each other. They also learned that the middle-aged runner was a puzzle expert and would gladly have offered her expertise.

There can be no doubt that Outward Bound training is not for everybody, but then nothing is. Some find out after signing up. A small percentage (under 4 percent) quit in the middle of the training because it is not what they expected it to be. For many others, the program results in beneficial self-awareness. In the words of a New York academic dean, "I couldn't believe the support and encouragement of my colleagues. They trusted me and I trusted them. This program unleashed a power I never knew I had."

Limitations of Training

Department chairs, deans, provosts, and presidents who have participated in development programs very often report that they resume their posts refreshed and excited about their newly acquired ideas and techniques. For some, however, enthusiasm quickly wanes when their institutions give their proposed changes only tepid reception.

Though the ideas and techniques learned in the development programs may be relevant, well presented, and useful, they are sometimes not put to work by administrators. The reasons? Some administrators are insufficiently motivated to implement what they have learned. Others object to outsiders telling them what to do, and still others are incapable of fitting what they have learned to their own institutions.

Shtogren (1978) and Seldin (1987) suggest dealing with such difficulties by (1) multiplying the specialized training resources that have "face validity," (2) acting more in a collaborative than in an instructional mode, (3) adapting training materials to the administrators' culture, and (4) providing sufficient institutional incentives to motivate administrators to apply the knowledge and techniques they have learned to their own institutions.

Evaluating Administrative Development Programs

There is precious little information currently available on the effectiveness of administrative development programs. The literature is skimpy and essentially anecdotal, and the reported studies are mostly simplistic. Thus, it is specially important for development programs to add an evaluation component that seeks answers to such questions as: What did you like about the program? What did you dislike? Do you feel the information was worthwhile? Was it presented in an interesting, meaningful, relevant way? Was the program well prepared and well organized?

Addressing the same point, Fisher and Coll-Pardo (1979) urge administrators about to select a development program to bear in mind certain questions: First, is there provision for participants to evaluate the learning experience at the program's conclusion or at some later point? Second, is there compelling evidence that these evaluations have confirmed certain facets of the program and led to the improvement of others?

The case-study method provides an in-depth exploration of what happened and what the outcomes appear to be, and it sometimes even suggests topics that need closer scrutiny. It comes up with specific effects believed to be caused by one or more factors in the program. The evaluation process then seeks the causative factors (Wergin, 1977). The utility of a case study clearly depends on the observer's astuteness and skills. Seasoned observers are needed to evaluate the sequential events in the program, as well as the program's effectiveness, and to prescribe necessary changes (Cherrington, 1987).

One commonly used evaluation model is the Context-Input-Process-Product (CIPP) developed by Daniel Stufflebeam. In this model, *context* determines the program objectives, which consist of "consumer" criteria, "competitor" criteria, and environmental factors. *Input* includes alternative plans and strategies. *Process* monitors implementation. *Product* measures and interprets both short- and long-term effects (Stordahl, 1981).

There are two additional techniques to evaluate professional development programs: (1) *judicial evaluation*, in which testimony is presented at an open hearing and a decision reached on the program's value by a cross section of the institution's community; and (2) *goal-free evaluation*, in which external consultants serve as evaluators without knowing the program's goals (Seldin, 1983).

Whatever the evaluation technique, it must be appropriate to the setting and situation. Behavioral change is a subtle and complex process. It must be evaluated sensitively and thoughtfully.

Conclusion

To dismiss efforts to improve administrative behavior by asserting that administrators must learn for themselves the requisite attitudes and behaviors is unrewarding and unacceptable. So is insistence that the learning process is too complex to be understood through analysis. Such claims are often self-serving. Equipped with hindsight and the benefit of research, we now know a great deal about the process of academic administration. We can identify not only the basic requirements of academic administration but also the subtle changes in attitudes and behaviors that strengthen performance. We can ill afford the wasteful trial-and-error learning of the past. On-the-job experience is certainly valuable, but it needs augmenting by professional development activities. A combination of the two is the fastest and most effective way to master the science and art of administration.

Because the process of administrative evaluation and development must begin with top-level administrators, the next chapter will examine the president as role model.

⊁ 8 ⊀

Evaluating and Developing the President: A Role Model for the Process

College and university presidents live very much in the public domain, and for good reason. No matter the size, complexity, or status of the institution, the president's decisions constantly affect its well-being. They also impinge on the lives of those who make up the educational community. The president's decisions are greeted with approval and disapproval, often with both. Faculty, students, trustees, staff, alumni, donors, state education officers, legislators, church officials, taxpayers, and local citizens have traditionally exercised their perceived right to pass judgment on the president's personality, attitudes, and performance, to say nothing of his or her decisions.

New Directions

But a fresh wind is blowing in presidential corridors these days. In the past decade the trend has been to formalize the presidential evaluation process. Casual, piecemeal, and limited-vision judgments by board members behind closed doors are being exchanged for a more public, systematic search for genuine evidence of a candidate's qualifications (Nason, 1984).

The final authority for reappointing or terminating the

president still resides with the board of regents or the trustees. But now, an advisory committee of faculty, administrators, students, staff personnel, alumni, and others usually assesses the president's performance. True, the advisory committee's judgments can be ignored, but that is not the way things work in this age of participatory democracy and shared governance.

The result is that today the college or university president serves not just "at the pleasure of the board" but at the pleasure of all the major constituencies on the campus, and of some constituencies (for example, alumni or the head of a statewide system) off campus (Arden, 1984).

Before discussing the evaluation and development of presidents, it may be helpful to offer a few generalizations about the presidency today and about the skills and characteristics frequently found in the more effective presidents.

The Presidency Today. When we discuss the presidency of an educational institution, we are talking about a wide variety of roles and tasks. The president of a community college district with three campuses must be differentiated from the presidents of the three campuses. The head of a state system must be differentiated from the presidents of the institutions within that system. The public institution presidency is different from the private institution presidency.

Despite these differences, college and university presidents share many things in common. All of them are expected to be divinely endowed. They are expected to possess the mental clarity of a Zen master, the determination of Atlas, the stamina of an Olympic runner, the tenderness of St. Francis, the creativity of Picasso. Webb (1986) says that each day in the life of a college president brings a flurry of new challenges. One day the president is an architectural consultant, a strategic planner, and a counselor; the next day, a marketing expert, referee, teacher, and financial analyst; and daily a scientist, humanist, and philosopher. Arden (1984) remarks that if one listens to public pronouncements, the president is supposed to do everything superbly and, if not walk on water, at least know where the rocks are. The president is supposed to be a savvy politician and at the same time a model of integrity and honesty; a strong, decisive leader guided by a special vision of the institution's future, as well as an impartial paragon who weighs all sides of an argument and invites full discussion of every issue. With such exaggerated expectations, says Arden, not even one of Plato's philosopher-kings should apply.

Kerr and Gade (1986) divide presidents into four categories: leaders, managers, survivors, and scapegoats. Leaders strive to make important changes, revolutionary or evolutionary, in existing institutions, as Charles W. Eliot did at Harvard during his tenure from 1869 to 1909, or as Wallace Sterling did at Stanford from 1949 to 1968. Managers seek to operate institutions at stepped-up efficiency, without drastic changes. This appeals to trustees who favor "nonthreatening" personalities. Survivors (or timeservers) tend to make it by their wits and lack of scruples. Scapegoats are useful to colleges and universities in trouble. If the price of survival is to do nothing, they willingly do nothing. Though morally questionable, scapegoating absolves the other actors of culpability and responsibility. Sacrifice the president and start over again.

In 1960, the average term of office for a college or university president was eleven years. Today, it is seven years. Why the rush to relinquish the seats of power? In the view of some, it is because grievances accumulate and fatigue sets in. Other observers think it results from conflict with board policies or board members (Huddleston, Kowalski, and Cangemi, 1984). For still other observers, say Kerr and Gade (1986), it is because presidential power has become an illusion. In return for the appearance of power, presidents must give up much of what appeals to them—scholarship (if they were previously respected scholars) or administrative influence (if they came from such academic positions as provost or dean).

In any case, they give up personal privacy. A. Bartlett Giamatti, former president of Yale University, put it this way: "You go from being a private person to suddenly reading descriptions of your face, your clothes, the way your hands look" (Hechinger, 1986, p. C12). Another former university president called it "a lonely life in a fishbowl."

Following a two-and-one-half-year study, the national

Commission on Strengthening Presidential Leadership concluded that American colleges and universities are suffering from a pervasive lack of strong presidential leadership. The basic problem, the commission said, is that the president's job at many institutions has become too difficult, too stressful, too constrained by outside influences, and too unrewarding to attract or long retain the kind of person who is probably best qualified to serve. In an interview with the *Chronicle of Higher Education*, Clark Kerr, head of the commission, underscored the commission's view that the leadership gap was more a function of constraining barriers surrounding the presidency than of the caliber of people currently serving in the office. What are the barriers? They include (1) more federal and state controls on academic institutions; (2) more faculty influence over appointments, promotions, and academic policy; (3) more student influence on campus governance; (4) more participation by boards of trustees in daily decision making; (5) less chance for institutions to grow and change; and (6) less acceptance of authority throughout society (Jacobson, 1984a).

Granted that these barriers to effectiveness have thwarted some presidents, others have managed to overcome them and have achieved national, even international, renown. To name a few:

- Derek Bok, Harvard University
- Richard M. Cyert, Carnegie Mellon University
- Colin G. Campbell, Wesleyan University
- Martha E. Church, Hood College
- Rhoda M. Dorsey, Goucher College
- A. Bartlett Giamatti, Yale University
- Hanna H. Gray, University of Chicago
- Joseph N. Hankin, Westchester Community College
- Theodore M. Hesburgh, Notre Dame University
- Robert H. McCabe, Miami-Dade Community College
- Sister Joel Read, Alverno College

Characteristics Shared by Most Effective Presidents. Reporting on the preliminary results of a study by Fisher and

Tack, McMillen (1986b) says that the most effective presidents (1) believe less in close collegial relationships than do "typical" presidents; (2) rely on respect rather than on popularity; (3) work longer hours, make decisions more easily, and confide less frequently in other presidents than do their counterparts in other institutions; (4) care about "little people" at the institution and demonstrate a strong element of humanity; and (5) are strong risk-taking loners with a dream. These characteristics actually do not threaten the idea of shared governance because these presidents firmly believe in it. But they also keep firmly in mind that they are the final authority. Fisher and Tack (1986), in a letter to the editor of the *Chronicle of Higher Education*, report finding statistically significant differences in the answers to the Fisher-Tack Effective Leadership Inventory between "effective" and "representative" presidents. This means, they say, that there is now an instrument that governing boards and potential presidents may find useful in predicting the effectiveness of future presidents.

Gilley, Fulmer, and Reithlingshoffer (1986), in a study of twenty successful institutions of higher education and their presidents, find that an institution that is growing and striving for academic excellence is likely to be headed by a president who cares for people, supports them, and nurtures them. This kind of president translates into action the idea that people make a difference. He or she (1) works well with governing board members, (2) exhibits dogged persistence in pursuit of goals, (3) keeps his or her antennae always extended, (4) demonstrates a sixth sense about opportunities, and (5) takes unexpected actions. (It should be added that this kind of president occasionally irritates mid-level administrators by sidestepping the chain of command to find solutions to vexing problems.)

Falvey (1982) adds a few touches of his own to the portrait of the effective president. The effective president tells specified subordinates the kind of accomplishments most desired and appreciated. While destructive criticism is eschewed, the flow of notes praising accomplishments is unceasing. In addition to writing notes, the effective president meets informally with subordinates to add verbal accolades for work well done.

Presidents who have the capacity to conceive and execute successful strategic plans share at least one more characteristic: the ability to think in a time span of years instead of months. This long-range conceptual framework is unusual and far exceeds the mental planning range of most people. Relatively few can visualize life in five-year increments, and only the most gifted can think in terms of a decade. In a sense, such conceptual ability resembles the mental processes and scope of a grand master who appreciates the significance of each chess move and relates it to the projected outcome of the game.

Advice for Trustees and Aspiring Presidents. The Commission on Strengthening Presidential Leadership, after interviewing nearly 850 presidents and other officials, suggests that aspiring presidents take careful stock of their abilities. Jacobson (1984b), a reporter for the *Chronicle of Higher Education*, writes that the commission advises such aspirants and the governing boards weighing their appointment to ask the following questions:

1. Do the candidates have the physical endurance and psychological resiliency that the presidency requires?
2. Are their family circumstances compatible with the job?
3. Are they willing to function in the midst of ambiguity and conflict?
4. Are they willing to inflict and accept personal pain for the sake of progress?
5. Are they patient enough for seemingly endless consultations and efforts at persuasion?
6. Are they willing to accept a changed relationship with faculty members—where friends may become acquaintances, and acquaintances may become critics?
7. Do their values, executive style, and abilities fit the particular institution and its current needs?

As a result of its readings and numerous interviews with long-term successful presidents and chancellors, the commission provides the following suggestions to would-be presidents: (1) don't promise too much in advance; (2) provide a vision and structure for what you promise; (3) walk the campus and listen a lot—the leg is better than the letter for carrying a message; (4) be ready to fight but only for what you are willing to die for; (5) don't give all your heart to the institution—you may lose it; (6) never surprise the governing board; (7) cultivate patience; (8) don't cackle like a hen every time you achieve something; (9) don't let routine work drive out nonroutine work; (10) convince your board members to keep their eyes, ears, and minds open—and their hands off; (11) save some time for laughter; and (12) be lucky in terms of time, place, and having a good governing board or a good chair on the board or both.

Evaluating the Performance of the President

Given the complexity of a college or university, it is important to assess the president's effectiveness in carrying out the duties of the office and the mission of the institution. In an ideal world, presidential self-assessment would be more than enough to identify areas that need improvement. In the imperfect world that we inhabit, however, it would be remarkable indeed for presidents, or anyone else, to come up with objective self-analyses. For that reason alone, more formal procedures invoking the judgment of others are needed.

Systematic evaluation need not be threatening or disruptive. It can, instead, help clear the air and generate the kind of support within an institution that innovative presidential leadership requires. One cautionary note: an evaluation is not something to be entered into lightly. Well done, it can be beneficial; poorly done, it can damage both president and institution. Much has to do with the approach. If the governing board signals that the goal is to improve performance, perhaps even the performance of the board itself, it will influence the president's attitude toward evaluation positively. That, in turn, will ensure a more effective assessment.

Purposes of Evaluation. The primary reasons to evaluate the president are (1) to determine that the institution is well managed, (2) to help the president improve his or her performance, (3) to improve institutional governance, (4) and to ensure that sound institutional goals are being pursued. As Ronald

Stead, former president of the Association of American Colleges, said, "The primary reason for a top-level evaluation should be to improve the performance of the president, the [governing] board, and the institution as a whole" ("AGB Special Report . . . ," 1983, p. 37).

A few secondary reasons to assess presidential performance are (1) to help determine whether to retain or terminate the president and (2) to help the governing board to find out what is going on. In the words of a former president of Colby College (Maine), "the most helpful result of presidential assessment is the further education of the board of trustees" (Strider, 1982, p. 54). Nason (1984, p. 29) agrees: "Periodic, full-dress assessments of institutional goals and administrative performance are almost the only ways by which trustees can feel reasonably certain how things are faring."

Another not inconsequential reason to review presidential performance is to set an example for evaluations of other administrators and faculty members. The president of Midland Lutheran College (Nebraska) comments: "In my fifteen years as a faculty member prior to assuming the presidency, I advocated and appreciated [student] evaluations. . . . Since I wanted to initiate [as president] a process of evaluation for administrators to augment [student evaluations], it seemed unfair and inconsistent not to include the president in the process" (Hansen, 1984, p. 6).

Robert Lisensky, former president of Willamette University (Oregon), observes that the evalution purpose must dovetail with the institution's character and goals within a prescribed time period. Presidents, he says, can benefit from both informal annual reviews and in-depth periodic assessments ("AGB Special Report . . . ," 1983).

What are the principal benefits of formal assessments? A carefully structured and regularly scheduled review of presidential performance can (1) provide a stage for the chief executive to explore the complexities of academic leadership; (2) demonstrate the capacity of the assessment system to address management problems, stimulate required changes, and strengthen performance, all of which refresh the institution-wide administrative process; (3) be responsive to the clamor for accountability in higher education; (4) create an interaction of selection and evaluation procedures that will direct institutional resources toward well-defined priorities and goals; (5) identify the specifics of presidential administration that require strengthening and propose a plan for improvement; (6) encourage a more supportive relationship between governing board and president and help both review institutional assumptions and priorities.

Objections to Evaluation. Despite the many patent benefits that result from the formal assessment of presidents, more than a few academics remain unconvinced. They perceive assessment as an obstacle to administrative leadership. Since there are some prominent names among the naysayers, their objections need serious consideration.

In his book devoted to the academic presidency, Kauffman (1980) argues that such evaluations actually do not accomplish much. Again, the president of the Council for Advancement and Support of Education, together with the president of the Council of Independent Colleges, sees formal presidential evaluations as possibly "the single greatest barrier to a healthy future for higher education" (Fisher and Quehl, 1984, p. 5). Tucker and Mautz (1979) are persuaded that the position of academic president is so varied, thorny, and mercurial that a measure of dissatisfaction with the president's performance is virtually inevitable, regardless of whether the incumbent is saint or sinner. David Reisman, a Harvard sociologist, believes that continual, short-term judgments of performance can serve as a lightning rod for grievances from faculty, students, staff, and alumni. In self-defense, presidents can become too timid (Kerr and Gade, 1986).

The arguments of these and other critics actually are twofold: presidential evaluation leads to a decline in the governing board's authority and to a decline in the president's authority. Discussing the first of these objections, Seldin (1987) argues that the board's power to make final decisions continues undiminished. Even in the preevaluation era, responsible governing boards sought discreet ways to tap the views of various constituencies on presidential performance. These quiet approaches have yielded to a more formal, systematic, and open process. As Arden (1984, p. 72) says, "If a board is so weak that it is undercut by a partially open and shared process, it would probably be less than adequate in exercising its authority. A strong board has nothing to fear."

As for the feared decline in the president's authority, this would represent a potent argument if true. The top administrator must be strong enough to act as role model to the institution's administrators and faculty. To Arden, however, the argument cuts both ways: "Precisely because strong leadership is crucial, we cannot afford the luxury of keeping ineffective presidents in office. Periodic assessments, if done intelligently, would be no threat to the presidents who are doing a good job; at the same time, the ones who are not could be identified and eliminated, making way for stronger successors" (p. 72).

The president of a midwestern liberal arts college put it this way: "I did a good job as president. I knew it. But the board didn't until they heard it from some administrators, faculty, alumni, and community leaders." A member of the board of governors of a southern university described the other side of the coin: "We were startled when we found out. How could we know the president was mismatched to our institution's needs. We found out through formal evaluation. So we replaced him. The new president is doing an excellent job."

Admittedly, the institution embarking on a presidential evaluation program is inviting risks. The program can degenerate into an academic circus or encourage a vendetta. It can turn into a spectacle of public humiliation and provide a convenient scapegoat for institutional failures. But an assessment distinguished by fairness and sensitivity is more likely to reinforce excellent performance and to help correct administrative weaknesses. The process can be invigorating to president and institution alike.

Methods for Evaluating Performance

Certain aspects of an academic presidency can be judged best—and perhaps only—by members of the governing board. But other judgments can and should be made by those directly impacted by the actions of the president. That is why, for example, the Board of Regents of The Pennsylvania State University includes the president's working relationship with faculty, students, and staff governance groups among presidential qualifications.

Some critics, of course, think that faculty, staff members, and students are not competent to evaluate a president. No doubt, in regard to certain presidential activities, such as building relationships with power brokers in state capitals, they lack the firsthand knowledge needed to make informed judgments. But in other cases—for example, in resolving grievances or working with campus constituencies—they are patently qualified.

Governing board members often find it troublesome to be asked to assess the president's performance. If their direct involvement with the president consists of not much more than reports generated for broad consumption, they may prefer to rely on other sources of information (Wood, 1984). Some rely on the student newspaper, others on the rumor mill. The majority, however, solicit the views of faculty members and senior administrators. Nason (1984, p. 48) argues that a "reasonably thorough and honest evaluation . . . must include opinions and attitudes from the various constituencies with whom the president works." Dennis and Bullerdieck (1986) agree.

The same questions should not be asked of all constituencies nor should answers be confused with votes. Academic presidents are selected, not elected. Nor does everyone have a "right" to be questioned.

Not surprisingly, the procedures employed to evaluate the president's performance vary widely, depending on the makeup of the governing board, the type and complexity of the institution, the campus climate, its different constituencies, and the time, energy, money expenditures that are institutionally acceptable.

In general, the review process begins with a statement from the president spelling out his or her objectives on assuming office and analyzing progress toward their achievement. This statement offers the president a chance to present his or her view of the leadership function and a rationale for the working style to meet the institution's character and needs. Meanwhile, the board (often working with an external adviser) identifies the social conditions within the institution and arrives at a set of assumptions concerning the president's role, thus fixing the frame of reference for the evaluation (Munitz, 1978). Since the board is responsible for a considerable number of academic matters, an advisory committee of a few board members plus others is normally appointed to oversee the evaluation.

McKenna (1972), Seldin (1983), and Shaw (1985) agree that the governing board should state exactly what it intends to accomplish by the review. The primary purpose should be to improve performance and not to determine whether the president should be retained or to fix compensation. It should be clear to everyone that the board is conducting the assessment as part of its overall responsibility and that both president and board stand to be beneficiaries.

Many methods are used by boards to determine the president's effectiveness. Among the favored techniques are personal interviews, user-group assessment, focus groups, self-evaluation, institutional analysis, and questionnaires. Not infrequently, the evaluation ranges over problem solving to presidential style.

Models of Presidential Evaluation

There is general agreement that the chosen method of evaluation must fit the character of the institution and the specific objectives set for the assessment. Seldin (1983) identifies four models of evaluation as (1) MBO, (2) the internal feedback system, (3) the ad hoc committee, and (4) the external consultant. Institutions generally use combinations of these models.

MBO. At the time of his or her initial appointment, the president and the institution must agree on the president's goals and objectives, since his or her effectiveness will eventually be measured by the degree to which these goals and objectives have been achieved. The president of Hampshire College (Massachusetts) describes her evaluation by a team of three trustees in this way: They "read with care my detailed report on major developments at the college in the last five years" and compared "the goals I set for myself and for the institution in my inaugural address" (Simmons, 1984, p. 4). Performance goals do change over time. These goals and other modifications need candid airing and should be discussed along with the president's reports to the governing board.

The MBO approach finds favor in institutions in which the president has an immediate supervisor, such as a chancellor. Jointly, they fix objectives that they then periodically review to measure progress.

Internal Feedback System. In this approach, the president's performance is reviewed by internal administrators, faculty members, students, alumni, and others. They judge perceived strengths and weaknesses, and their judgments are usually coordinated by an assessment committee.

At Augsburg College (Minnesota), for example, by agreement with the board of regents, the president is evaluated the second, third, and fifth year of a six-year term. The evaluation questionnaire is typically sent to more than 150 people, including (1) administrators who report directly to the president and those who do not, (2) faculty, (3) maintenance/clerical personnel, (4) students, (5) alumni, and (6) parents. In addition, large numbers of individuals from the on-campus and off-campus communities are interviewed by committee members assigned by the board of regents.

Ad Hoc Committees. Here, the focus is on the development of an evaluation portfolio. Since this process requires the president to state his or her understanding of the institution's objectives and to specify the degree to which they have been achieved, self-assessment becomes the backbone of the evaluation. The ad hoc committee formulates the statements of the groupings represented on it and their consensus judgment on the president's performance. Hall (1979) and Seldin (1984) report that an offshoot of this procedure, which is particularly appropriate for large institutions, is the use of different committees to represent different constituencies. Each committee's report summarizes its constituency's views. The State University of New York has utilized the ad hoc committee approach.

External Consultants. Many institutions employ an external consultant to advise and assist in the presidential evaluation.

The reason is that the observer-facilitator-interpreter can encourage objectivity, reconcile disputes, defuse political rivalries, and exercise the kind of authority needed to establish guidelines for board recommendations. An authoritative outsider is in a good position to create trust, provide comfort, relieve tension, and reduce conflict—all necessary ingredients for reliable evaluation (Munitz, 1978). In addition, the consultant can offer board members a fresh view on how the campus is working.

Time and money can be saved when the board employs a professional who has gained experience at many institutions and who knows the latest techniques in presidential assessment. The president also stands to benefit because the consultant is a disinterested third party with whom discussions can be pursued in confidence.

An outside consultant is not, of course, a prerequisite to an effective evaluation, but use of such a consultant can be especially helpful given four circumstances: (1) when the board is somewhat inexperienced in appraisals, (2) when the board simply lacks the time to conduct a proper evaluation, (3) when the board decides on direct interviewing as a means of evaluating the president and needs someone to ask the right questions who does not have a vested interest in the answers, and (4) when the need arises at the completion of the evaluation for an outsider to talk objectively with the governing board's head or the president about issues that are particularly sensitive and personal ("AGB Special Report . . . ," 1983). An outside consultant can also be helpful when the board wants a presidential evaluation in which faculty, students, administrators, alumni, and others provide data but do not serve on the evaluation committee.

It is a truism that colleges and universities differ in mission, values, and time-honored ways of doing things. What works well at one institution may fizzle at another. Even so, it may prove salutary to know in some detail the evaluative process at another institution. Consider, then, the approach at one midwestern university:

Southeast Missouri State University. Initiating the formal review process, the head of the board of regents sends a packet to employees, alumni, and students of the university, as well as community leaders and area legislators. The packet contains (1) a two-page description of the role and responsibility of the president, (2) a forty-question survey and response scan sheet, and (3) a copy of the president's vita. A covering letter explains the purpose of the review, assures respondents of confidentiality, and requests return of the completed forms within two weeks. A reply envelope addressed to the Office of Institutional Research is enclosed.

Directions ask respondents to read the materials carefully before replying. As a help in analyzing replies, the respondents are asked to state their years of service at the university and their position or rank (for example, administrator, instructor/assistant professor, associate/full professor, support professional, maintenance, clerical, student). They are directed to rate the president's performance on a continuum of one to seven and to omit any question for which they lack an adequate basis to respond. The questions address the following areas: academic administration and planning, budgetary and fiscal management, communication, decision making and problem solving, external relations, and personnel. In the blank space on the reverse of the scan sheet, respondents are asked two additional questions: (1) What makes the president an effective administrator? (2) How do you feel the president could improve his or her effectiveness? The main purpose of the review is to examine the ability of the president to enhance the institution. The approach is comprehensive, thoughtful, and sensitive.

Criteria for Evaluating the President

In interviews, Kauffman (1978) asked respondents completing their first year in office to identify the criteria on which their successes and failures would be judged. Most presidents were unclear as to which criteria would be used. Nothing commends such ignorance. It is critical to have genuine, two-way communication between president and governing board about specific institutional and personal goals and evaluative criteria. As the president of a West Coast college stated: "It is vital to have a mutual understanding between the incoming president and the board at the time of appointment. What are the major goals the board expects the president to achieve in the first two years? In five years? Open and honest communication is a must if realistic criteria are to be set up."

Nationally, what are the high-priority items of academic presidents? In a survey of 900 college and university presidents, Patrick and Caruthers (1980) found that they accord highest priority to (1) communicating the institution's strengths to prospective students, their parents, and the general public; (2) communicating the institution's strengths to state legislators and other government officials; (3) integrating the findings of program reviews into program planning and budget processes; (4) allocating and reallocating resources; (5) encouraging faculty renewal; (6) implementing the institution's objectives by planning and budgeting; and (7) accurately forecasting institutional revenues.

Not surprisingly, these presidential priorities largely overlap the criteria used to evaluate presidents. A review of questionnaires used in institutions varying in size, mission, and prestige indicates that the criteria generally fall into the following categories:

- Administration and Management—including academic planning, program planning, decision making, problem solving, use of funds, facilities, and human resources.
- Leadership—including leadership of various publics, the governing board, faculty, students, and other institutional presidents.
- Personal Qualities—including integrity, confidence, tolerance, tact, persuasiveness, fairness, flexibility, concern for quality, and sensitivity.

Bok (1986) notes that presidents also have an opportunity to shape the academic agenda and create an environment that promotes innovation and supports new ideas. This, too, is a criterion frequently found, in one form or another, in presidential assessments.

If all the criteria listed here as essential for an academic president were strictly applied, it would probably eliminate the species. No institution can seriously expect such exemplary performance. Nor does any institution need it. The practical way to develop a list of presidential criteria is to tailor it to the institution's mission, values, and traditions, as well as to the concrete objectives to which the president is expected to give priority. And always keep the criteria in the forefront as a checklist when eliciting information. This checklist can serve as a mental guide when the president's performance is being discussed. Needless to say, the criteria must be sufficiently refined so as to address not the general (what *any* president does at *any* institution) but the specific (what *this* president does at *this* institution).

Fairness requires that the president receive, or have access to, all evaluative information except that which by prior agreement is to remain confidential. The latter category is best kept as close to zero as possible. There are times when an institution has compelling reasons to keep some data confidential, but this should be an exception to the general rule of full disclosure.

Generally, the president should have access to all evaluative data and their general sources. Written or oral evaluative comments should be summarized or given verbatim without identifying the originating individual. When asked for information, respondents must be guaranteed anonymity. Generally, also, the respondents should receive, or have access to, the overall results from their group but not necessarily from other groups. Special circumstances may make advisable full disclosure of all summarized information to all respondents and even other interested parties, except perhaps for information about sensitive personal matters. Conceivably, that might happen if full disclosure produces a turnabout institutional climate of mutual trust and respect. A compromise between disclosure and confidentiality might be to keep evaluation details confidential and go public with an interpretation of the general findings (Cleveland, 1985). The obvious benefit is to avoid personalizing and focus on the broad issues.

Professional Development of the President

The primary goal of a formal, systematic evaluation of the president's performance should be improvement of that performance. Obviously, however, a president needs a great deal of information about his past and current performance if he is to change it for the better. The word *dissonance* suggests itself here. Feedback can and should produce in the president a kind of dissonance or dissatisfaction that sets the psychological stage for change.

Whether the president's performance actually improves, however, depends in large measure on what turns up in the evaluation. There is likely to be little progress unless the areas to be improved are specified. And even then, the president must genuinely support the evaluative process and be capable of making the changes needed to produce improvement.

What areas of improvement are likely to emerge from a presidential evaluation? They vary from person to person but generally include (1) administrative style, (2) relationships with faculty and others, (3) decision making and problem solving, (4) strategic planning, (5) communication, and (6) fiscal management.

A few examples follow to illustrate these points. A midwestern college president reports that her evaluation suggested that she strengthen her performance by (1) being less defensive when her viewpoint is challenged, (2) being more careful to follow the chain of command, (3) building a better-knit administrative team, (4) adopting a more participative management style, and (5) increasing her knowledge of fiscal matters.

A president of a western college learned from his evaluation that he should (1) develop a more positive public image, (2) interact more frequently with faculty and students, (3) gain more knowledge of long-range planning and fiscal management, and (4) change his autocratic leadership style.

An eastern college president found out that he should (1) develop a team administration, (2) take more academic risks, (3) learn to translate policy into action, and (4) quit publicly recounting how he handled things as president of a different college.

A few administrative weaknesses can be eliminated on the spot simply by identifying them. But most require participation in one or more professional growth activities. There are many options available to presidents who want to beef up their performance. They include developing a professional growth plan, taking a sabbatical or administrative leave, or attending conferences and seminars.

Developing a Professional Growth Plan. McKenna (1972) points out that once the decision to hire a president has been made, most governing boards breathe a sigh of relief and in effect abandon the president to his or her fate. Yet the post-decision care and feeding of the president is certainly as important as his or her selection. McKenna recommends that the board initiate a professional growth plan for the president to encourage that officer to pursue his or her special interests in research, writing, public service, consulting, or travel. The pursuit of special interests may have no direct or immediate return for the institution but should nonetheless be undertaken.

As part of a growth plan, for instance, the president of a college in Arkansas suggested to his governing board that he could enhance his leadership role by foreign travel. The governing board supported his proposal and funded his trip to the People's Republic of China (Brown, 1984).

Sabbaticals. After four or five grueling years in office, many presidents feel shopworn, frayed around the edges, or receive a hard-to-turn-down offer. In anticipation, many institutions provide for periodic sabbaticals. Generally running from two to six months, the sabbaticals are geared to the professional development and personal growth of the presidents, with an eye to the future needs of the institutions.

Some institutions provide a two-month sabbatical at full salary after three years of service and a one-semester sabbatical at full salary after five years. Among the presidents recently awarded sabbaticals are Derek Bok (Harvard University) and Paul Hardin (Drew University, New Jersey).

Attending Conferences and Seminars. Although many presidents deal with administrative weaknesses through professional growth plans or sabbaticals, most take a different route. They attend professional conferences and seminars. They do so essentially for two reasons: to pick up content knowledge and to share problems of mutual concern.

Several programs hold special pertinence for college and university presidents. One is "The Effective CEO: A Seminar on Presidential Leadership." This four-day annual seminar, sponsored by the American Council on Education (ACE), focuses on issues of leadership. The 1987 curriculum covered (1) the joys and sorrows of the presidency, (2) national issues in higher education, (3) financial management for private and public institutions, (4) the changing scene in postsecondary education, (5) building a governing board, (6) working with the media, (7) the presidential role in development, (8) external relations, (9) building a presidential team, and (10) presidential leadership. The curriculum is handled by prominent speakers and is based on small-group discussion. The fee for the program is $575 for presidents of ACE member institutions and $675 for presidents of nonmember institutions.

A unique feature of the program is that it gives participants the opportunity to improve their public speaking and relationship with the media through videotaping and individual coaching. Also available are optional sessions that allow participants to analyze financial aid at their own institutions and to work with a computer model using their own institutional data. The seminar is specially recommended to presidents in their first three years of office.

"Higher Education and the Law" is a one-and-one-half-day conference sponsored by the University of Georgia's Center for Continuing Education that discusses judicial decisions and trends in connection with academic decision making. The conference fee is $100. The 1987 conference covered the following issues:

- What legal liabilities face institutions and administrators?
- With regard to AIDS and other communicable diseases on campus, what are the potential legal liabilities?
- What are the parameters involving employment issues, including drug testing?
- What are the liabilities regarding copyright issues?

- What national issues are affecting the legal atmosphere on campus?
- How do courts define the legal issues in student life and academic affairs?
- How should administrators respond to drugs and alcohol on campus?

"A System of Strategic Planning for Higher Education" is a one-day workshop sponsored by Strategic Planning/Management Associates, Inc., of Topeka, Kansas. The cost is $250, and the curriculum includes: (1) the role of the president in strategic planning; (2) organizing for the planning process; (3) management information systems and costing; (4) external environment assessment; (5) education industry assessment; (6) competitor assessment; (7) program/market assessment; (8) analytical techniques—external environment; (9) institutional self-assessment; (10) human dimensions in strategic planning; (11) financial and facilities assessment; (12) analytical techniques—internal environment; (13) institutional mission, objectives, and goals; (14) strategies, action plans, and priorities; (15) strategic funds planning; and (16) contingency planning.

"Enhancing the Academic Workplace" is a two-day seminar conducted by the National Center for Higher Education Management Services. The cost is $400. The seminar analyzes the institution as a workplace and offers insights on faculty and administrator perceptions of work-related issues and how these perceptions affect performance. The curriculum includes the following topics: (1) an analysis of the workplace, including the extent of participation, commitment and loyalty to the institution, productivity, and satisfaction and morale; (2) external factors influencing the workplace; (3) actions needed to improve the work experience of faculty and administrators; and (4) models for implementing change. The seminar participants are encouraged to share their ideas and strategies with each other and to discuss their particular situations when the appropriate topic comes up.

Rather than focus on a central theme, some professional development programs take a more comprehensive approach.

An example is the Harvard University Institute for Educational Management (IEM), a four-week residential program for presidents (plus some vice-presidents and deans). The fee is $6,000. The curriculum covers the major challenges confronting senior academic officers: monitoring the environment, fixing institutional directions, marshaling resources and support, and managing implementation. Much of the curriculum, enhanced by prominent speakers, is based on the case method and small-group discussion. In 1987, some of the major program topics were (1) the relationship of professional and private life, (2) leadership and organizational behavior, (3) financial management and control, (4) academic personnel policy and administration, (5) small-group leadership, (6) institutional advancement, (7) political process, (8) minority status and issues in higher education, (9) labor relations and negotiations, (10) marketing concept, and (11) law and higher education. Admission to the IEM program is by application and the competition is stiff.

Conclusion

If it is true that a major issue confronting institutions of higher education is the recruitment and support of the best staff, then presidential evaluation that leads to improved performance and professional development makes sense on every campus. Governing boards owe it to themselves to protect the time and energy that they spend selecting a president. The institution and the president are best served by helping the president grow on the job.

In the words of a president from a southern university: "I learned during the evaluation some important things about myself, the politics of this institution, the perceptions of my colleagues. The negative feedback was painful. But I got some insights into needed changes, and I will make them. There was also a good deal of positive feedback. And it helped offset the negative. I can't say I 'enjoyed' the evaluation, and I'm glad it's over. But I benefited and so will the university."

To these words only one more needs to be added: Amen.

Appendix
Benchmarks for Evaluating and Developing Administrative Performance

The following lists of benchmarks are presented instead of a chapter-by-chapter summation. The lists represent some key points to consider in evaluating and developing the performance of today's academic administrators. An advisory note is in order: the full meaning of each of these points can best be understood and appreciated by reading the chapters themselves.

Chapter One: Changing Expectations and Roles of Academic Administrators

1. Evaluating and developing the performance of the new breed of administrator are essential to the improvement of campus management.
2. The primary reason to evaluate administrative performance systematically should be to improve it.
3. Formal, objective standards should displace personal biases in judging performance.
4. The process and procedures employed to assess an administrator on one level may be inappropriate for assessing an administrator on a different level.
5. The approaches selected for evaluation and development

213

should depend on such factors as level of position, type of institution, motivation of the individual, and available time and funds.

6. The methods selected to evaluate and develop academic administrators should be an outgrowth of the academic culture of the institution.

Chapter Two: Why Assess Administrative Performance?

1. Administrators should know accurately and completely the performance standards by which they will be evaluated.
2. Performance evaluations should not be restricted to one or two administrative functions. Such areas as planning, decision making, ability to deal with people, communication skills, initiative, adaptability, problem solving, and leadership might be included.
3. For a three-dimensional picture of the administrator, a wide range of sources for data should be utilized.
4. The program should include "upward" evaluation so that faculty members who have worked with administrators can participate in evaluating their performance.
5. The program should take into account the tendency of academic administrators to perceive performance appraisal as an implicit threat.
6. Resistance to the program should be overcome not by muscle but by listening to others' suggestions, trying to understand different points of view, explaining rather than arguing, modifying the program when appropriate, and not hurrying its acceptance.

Chapter Three: Evaluating Administrative Performance: What Works and What Doesn't

1. The first step in evaluating performance should be to scrutinize job descriptions and to develop new ones as needed. If they are more than two or three years old, they probably require an update.
2. All relevant components of an administrator's performance should be identified and included in the evaluation system.

Even components that are time consuming to evaluate or tend to defy measurement should be included.

3. Institutions should not give sole responsibility for performance appraisal to the administrator's immediate supervisor.
4. Appraisal instruments should be readily understood and easily put to use by administrators, faculty, staff, students, and others involved in the process.
5. Raters should be encouraged to omit responses when they feel unqualified to make judgments.
6. Institutions should understand there are many ways, not a single way, to evaluate administrative performance.

Chapter Four: Planning, Implementing, and Managing a Successful Evaluation Program

1. Even though supervisors may be excellent sources of evaluative data, institutions should include other appropriate raters so that the performance judgment rests on a broad base.
2. College and university presidents, academic vice-presidents, deans, and department chairs regularly interact with faculty members and should be evaluated by them.
3. Unsigned evaluations should be used.
4. Institutions should bear in mind that *how* an evaluation system is put into place is just as critical as *what* system is used. Introducing the program by presidential fiat foredooms it.
5. As a general rule, the administrator being assessed should have ready access to all evaluative information, except that which by prior agreement is to remain confidential.
6. After the program is implemented, it should be periodically reevaluated and fine tuned.

Chapter Five: Ensuring a Sound Legal Basis for Evaluation Activities

1. An institution's procedures for making and reviewing personnel decisions should be in writing and should be made public.

2. When reviewing administrative evaluation practices, colleges and universities should pay close attention to due process.
3. In the construction and review of evaluation procedures, institutions should consider procedural safeguards *before* making personnel decisions.
4. Legal counsel employed by institutions should have current knowledge of legal issues both in academic management and in affirmative action and EEOC guidelines.
5. Institutions should bear in mind that courts are primarily guardians of process. Courts are more reluctant to become involved in disputes over the substance of standards and criteria than in disputes over procedures for enforcing the standards and criteria.
6. Institutions should be aware of a new type of legal need— preventive law—that focuses on institutional initiatives to be taken *before* legal disputes arise.

Chapter Six: Strategies for Developing and Improving Administrative Performance

1. Performance evaluation should serve as a springboard for performance improvement.
2. All colleges and universities have some administrators with special expertise. These administrators should be identified and persuaded to share their expertise with their colleagues.
3. Learning the art and science of administration should be seen as a continuing process, achieved most effectively by a combination of day-to-day experience and administrator development activities.
4. Top-level administrators should support the program vocally, publicly, and with budgetary dollars.
5. Incentives should be offered to motivate administrators to continue practicing their newly learned skills and behaviors.
6. Colleges and universities should recognize that there is no unique formula for strengthening performance. The approach must be situational. The "right" approach today may be the "wrong" one in five years.

Chapter Seven: Providing Opportunities for Professional Development On and Off Campus

1. Institutions with skimpy budgets should consider some of the available no-cost or low-cost administrator development programs.
2. Senior administrators should help develop the skills and attitudes of less experienced administrators.
3. Institutions should be aware of international visitation schemes that offer administrators the opportunity to view key managerial issues from various perspectives.
4. Colleges and universities should look into Outward Bound training, which offers a unique approach to professional development. Its premise is that administrators learn better by actually doing rather than by attending workshops or reading books.
5. Administrator development programs should include an evaluative component that seeks answers to such questions as: What did you like about the program? Was it well prepared and well organized? Do you feel that the information presented was worthwhile?

Chapter Eight: Evaluating and Developing the President: A Role Model for the Process

1. An institution should not initiate an evaluation of its president without thoughtful preparation. Well done, such an evaluation can be beneficial; poorly done, it can damage both president and institution.
2. An important reason to review presidential performance should be to set an example for evaluations of other administrators.
3. The selected method of presidential evaluation should fit the character of the institution and the specific objectives set for the assessment.
4. Institutions should develop a list of presidential criteria by tailoring the evaluation to the college's or university's mis-

sion, values, and traditions, as well as to the concrete objectives to which the president is expected to give priority.

5. The same questions should not be asked of all constituencies nor should answers be confused with votes. Academic presidents are selected, not elected.

6. The review process should start with a statement from the president spelling out his or her objectives on assuming office and analyzing progress toward their achievement.

7. Presidential evaluation—like all administrator evaluation—should lead to improved performance and professional development.

References

"Academic Administrator Development." *University Education News*, 1982, *2* (4), 1–32.

ACE Fellows Program Information Brochure. Washington, D.C.: Center for Leadership Development, American Council on Education, 1987–1988.

"AGB Special Report—Presidential Assessments: A Roundtable Discussion." *AGB Reports*, Jan./Feb. 1983, pp. 36–41.

Allen, A. P. "The Relationships of Growth Contracting to Levels of Financial Support: A Case History." Unpublished doctoral dissertation, Department of Higher Education, University of Oklahoma, 1986.

American Association of State Colleges and Universities. *Program Evaluation.* Washington, D.C.: American Association of State Colleges and Universities, 1976.

Anderson, L. G. *The Evaluation of Academic Administrators: Principles, Process, and Outcomes.* University Park: Pennsylvania State University, 1975.

Arden, E. "Reviewing the Performance of College Presidents." *Chronicle of Higher Education*, Sept. 12, 1984, p. 72.

Austin, A. E., and Gamson, Z. F. *Academic Workplace: New Demands, Heightened Tensions.* ASHE-ERIC Higher Education Research Report, no. 10. Washington, D.C.: Association for the Study of Higher Education, 1983.

Bauer, R. C. *Cases in College Administration.* New York: Teachers College Press, 1955.

219

Baum, E. "The Appointment, Evaluation, and Termination of Academic Administrators." *AAHE Bulletin*, 1979, *32* (1), 9–12.

Beckham, J. C. *Faculty/Staff Nonrenewal and Dismissal for Cause in Institutions of Higher Education.* Asheville, N.C.: College Administration Publications, 1986.

Bedsole, D. T. "Austin College: Institution-Wide Career Development." In C. H. Farmer (ed.), *Administrative Evaluation: Concepts, Methods, Cases in Higher Education.* Richmond, Va.: Higher Education Leadership and Management Society, 1979.

Behling, O., and Darrow, A. L. *Managing Work-Related Stress.* Chicago: Science Research Association, 1984.

Beidler, P. G. "Some Advice for Would-Be Administrators from a Professor Who's Been There." *Chronicle of Higher Education*, Mar. 21, 1984, p. 96.

Bennett, J. B. *Managing the Academic Department.* New York: Macmillan, 1983.

Bennis, W. G. "An O.D. Expert in the Catbird Seat." *Journal of Higher Education*, 1973, *44*, 389–398.

Bergquist, W. H., and Tenbrink, G. J. "Evaluation of Administrators." In A. S. Knowles (ed.), *The International Encyclopedia of Higher Education.* Vol. 4. San Francisco: Jossey-Bass, 1977.

Berkshire, J. R., and Highland, R. W. "Forced-Choice Performance Rating: A Methodological Study." *Personnel Psychology*, 1953, *6*, 355–378.

Bernardin, H. J., and Beatty, R. W. *Performance Appraisal: Assessing Human Behavior at Work.* Boston: Kent, 1984.

Bickel, R. D. "Evaluation of Staff." *The College Administrator and the Courts* (quarterly supplement), 1978, *1* (3), 25.

Bickel, R. D. "Open Meetings Law (Missouri)." *The College Administrator and the Courts* (quarterly supplement), 1984, 7 (3), 292.

Bickel, R. D. "Administrative Employment." *The College Administrator and the Courts* (quarterly supplement), 1986, *9* (1), 365.

Bickel, R. D., and Brechner, J. A. *The College Administrator and the Courts*. Asheville, N.C.: College Administration Publications, 1978.

Birnbaum, R. "Leadership and Learning: The College President as Intuitive Scientist." *Review of Higher Education*, 1986, *9* (4), 381–395.

Black, D. "Using Legal Counsel." *Perspective: The Campus Legal Monthly*, 1986a, *3*, 3.

Black, D. "When You Even Think You're Going to Be Sued." *Perspective: The Campus Legal Monthly*, 1986b, *1* (6), 1.

Black, D. "Uncomplimentary Recommendations Draw Lawsuits." *Perspective: The Campus Legal Monthly*, 1987, *2* (5), 3.

Blom, D. I. "Management Training for University Administrators." *Journal of Staff, Program, and Organization Development*, 1985, *3* (2), 58–63.

Bok, D. *Higher Learning*. Cambridge, Mass.: Harvard University Press, 1986.

Bolman, F. "Can We Prepare Better College and University Administrators?" *Current Issues in Higher Education: 1964*. Washington, D.C.: American Association for Higher Education, 1964.

Booth, D. B. *The Department Chair: Professional Development and Role Conflict*. AAHE-ERIC Higher Education Report, no. 10. Washington, D.C.: American Association for Higher Education, 1982.

Bornholdt, L. "Evaluating the Evaluators." Paper presented at annual meeting of the American Conference of Academic Deans, Grand Forks, N.D., Feb. 1978.

Boulding, K. E. "The Management of Decline." *AGB Reports*, Sept./Oct. 1975, pp. 4–9.

Boyer, E. L. "Creative Management." Paper presented at the annual meeting of the *American Council on Education*, San Diego, Calif., Oct. 1974.

Boyer, R. K., and Grasha, A. F. "Theoretical Issues and Practical Strategies for Administrative Development." In J. A. Shtogren (ed.), *Administrative Development in Higher Education*. Richmond, Va.: Higher Education Leadership and Management Society, 1978.

Brett, R., and Fredian, A. J. "Performance Appraisal: The System Is Not the Solution." *Personnel Administrator*, 1981, *26*, 61–68.

Brookshire, M. L., and Tally, E. H. "Management Development and Training in Higher Education—the HEMI Project." *Journal of the College and University Personnel Association*, 1978, *29*, 35–46.

Brown, J. E. "Letter to the Editor." *Change*, Sept. 1984, p. 4.

Buchtel, F. "Approaches of Medium-Sized Universities." In P. Jedamus, M. W. Peterson, and Associates, *Improving Academic Management: A Handbook of Planning and Institutional Research.* San Francisco: Jossey-Bass, 1980.

Budig, G. A. "Presidential Opinions on Today's Key Issues." *AGB Reports*, 1986, *28*, 22–23.

Campbell, D. F. "A Linkages Model for Leadership Renewal." *Journal of Staff, Program, and Organization Development*, 1986, *4* (1), 21–25.

Campbell, D. P. "Inklings." *Issues and Observations*, 1987, 7 (1), 8–9.

Carter, L. K. "Cultivating Culture." *Currents*, June 1986, pp. 25–29.

Cascio, W. *Managing Human Resources.* New York: McGraw-Hill, 1986.

Cheit, E. "The Management Systems Challenge: How to Be Academic Though Systematic." In J. Hughes (ed.), *Education and the State.* Washington, D.C.: American Council on Education, 1975.

Cherrington, D. *Personnel Management.* Dubuque, Iowa: William C. Brown, 1987.

Cleveland, H. "Sunshine Laws and the 'Trilemma' They Present." *AGB Reports*, 1985, *27*, 18–20.

"Colorado Mountain College Fires Its President." *Chronicle of Higher Education*, June 11, 1986, p. 2.

Cousins, A. N., and Rogus, J. F. "Evaluating Academic Administrators—From Below." *Liberal Education*, 1977, *63*, 91–101.

Crow, M. L., and others. *Faculty Development Centers in Southern Universities.* Atlanta: Southern Regional Education Board, 1976.

Culbertson, J. "International Networking: Expanded Vistas for Leadership." *Theory into Practice*, 1981, *20* (4), 278–284.

Daloz, L. A. *Effective Teaching and Mentoring: Realizing the Transformational Power of Adult Learning Experiences.* San Francisco: Jossey-Bass, 1986.

Davis, K., and Newstrom, J. W. *Human Behavior at Work: Organizational Behavior.* New York: McGraw-Hill, 1985.

Dennis, L. J., and Bullerdieck, K. "Faculty Role in Presidential Evaluation." *College and University Personnel Association*, 1986, *37* (3), 1–4.

DeVries, D. L., and others. *Performance Appraisal on the Line.* Greensboro, N.C.: Center for Creative Leadership, 1986.

Douglas, L. H. "In Search of Excellence on College Campuses." *Chronicle of Higher Education*, Sept. 19, 1984, p. 72.

Dressel, P. L. *Handbook of Academic Evaluation: Assessing Institutional Effectiveness, Student Progress, and Professional Performance for Decision Making in Higher Education.* San Francisco: Jossey-Bass, 1976.

Dyer, W. G. "Managing Profiling: A Disparity Model for Developing Motivation for Change." Paper presented at the New Technology in Organization Development Conference, New Orleans, Feb. 1974.

Eble, K. *The Art of Administration: A Guide for Academic Administrators.* San Francisco: Jossey-Bass, 1978.

Edwards, C. W., and Pruyne, J. W. *The Administrator in Higher Education: An Assessment of Professional Needs.* Normal: Illinois State University and the University Council for Educational Administration, 1976.

Ehrle, E. B. "Selection and Evaluation of Department Chairmen." *Educational Record*, 1975, *56*, 29–38.

Falvey, J. "A Simple Strategy for Success." *Wall Street Journal*, Dec. 6, 1982, p. 30.

Farmer, C. H. "The Faculty Role in Administrative Evaluation." In C. F. Fisher (ed.), *Developing and Evaluating Administrative Leadership.* New Directions for Higher Education, no. 22. San Francisco: Jossey-Bass, 1978.

Farmer, C. H. *Administrator Evaluation: Concepts, Methods, Cases in Higher Education.* Richmond, Va.: Higher Education Leadership and Management Society, 1979.

Fields, C. M. "Academe's Increased Reliance on Legal Advice Documented by College Attorney's Association." *Chronicle of Higher Education,* July 17, 1985, p. 15.

Fisher, C. D. "Transmission of Positive and Negative Feedback to Subordinates: A Laboratory Study." *Journal of Applied Psychology,* 1979, *64* (4), 533–540.

Fisher, C. F. "The Evaluation and Development of College and University Administrators." *Research Currents,* Mar. 1977, pp. 3–6.

Fisher, C. F. "Improving Leadership: Selection, Evaluation, and Development of Administrators in Higher Education." In M. W. Peterson and L. A. Mets (eds.), *Key Resources on Higher Education Governance, Management, and Leadership: A Guide to the Literature.* San Francisco: Jossey-Bass, 1987.

Fisher, C. F., and Coll-Pardo, I. *Guide to Leadership Development Opportunities for College and University Administrators.* Washington, D.C.: American Council on Education, 1979.

Fisher, J. L., and Quehl, G. H. "Presidential Assessment: Obstacle to Leadership." *Change,* May/June 1984, pp. 5–7.

Fisher, J. L., and Tack, M. W. "Letter to the Editor." *Chronicle of Higher Education,* Dec. 3, 1986, p. 43.

Fisher, M. B., and Howell, J. A. "Evaluation and Accountability." *NASPA Journal,* 1972, *10,* 118–123.

"Five-Year Evaluation Planned for California State Presidents." *Chronicle of Higher Education,* Sept. 21, 1983, p. 3.

"Former Dean Sues Tennessee Regents. Charges Bias." *Chronicle of Higher Education,* Sept. 16, 1987, p. A16.

Fowler, E. M. "Outward Bound for Executives." *New York Times,* Aug. 1, 1984, p. 45.

Gaff, J. G. *Toward Faculty Renewal.* San Francisco: Jossey-Bass, 1975.

Gaff, S. S., Festa, C., and Gaff, J. G. *Professional Development: A Guide to Resources.* New York: Change Magazine Press, 1978.

Gatewood, R. D., and Feild, H. S. *Human Resources Selection.* Chicago: Dryden, 1987.

Genova, W. J., and others. *Mutual Benefit Evaluation of Fac-*

ulty and Administrators in Higher Education. Cambridge, Mass.: Ballinger, 1976.

Gilley, J. W., Fulmer, K. A., and Reithlingshoffer, S. J. *Searching for Academic Excellence.* New York: Macmillan, 1986.

Green, M. F. "Presidential Leadership: Changes in Style." *AGB Reports,* 1986, *28* (1), 18–20.

Hall, A. "Evaluation Commends, Criticizes Ryan." *Indiana Daily Student,* 1979, *111,* 1.

Hall, R. A., and Alfred, R. L. "Applied Research on Leadership in Community Colleges." *Community College Review,* 1985, *12,* 36–41.

Hansen, C. L. "It Seemed Like a Good Idea at the Time." *Change,* Sept. 1984, p. 6.

Hechinger, F. M. "Short Tenures Reflect Troubles of College Chiefs." *New York Times,* Mar. 18, 1986, p. C12.

Heller, J. F. *Increasing Faculty and Administrative Effectiveness.* San Francisco: Jossey-Bass, 1982.

Heller, S. "A National Center to Settle Campus Disputes Is Proposed." *Chronicle of Higher Education,* Oct. 1, 1986, p. 13.

Henderson, A. D. *Training University Administrators: A Program Guide.* Paris: UNESCO, 1970.

Hillway, T. "Evaluating College and University Administrators." *Intellect,* 1973, *101,* 426–427.

Horn, J. C. "Executive Action." *Psychology Today,* Jan. 1986, p. 14.

Hoyle, J. R. "To Evaluate a Dean." *Intellect,* 1973, *102,* 96–97.

Huddleston, R., Kowalski, C., and Cangemi, J. P. "Life Is Not Easy at the Top: The College President." *Psychology,* 1984, *21* (3/4), 31–34.

Hughes, M. G. "Educational Administration: Trends and Issues." *Members Newsletter* (College of Preceptors, England), Feb. 1987, pp. 23–43.

Ivancevich, J. M. "A Longitudinal Study of the Effects of Rater Training on Psychosomatic Errors in Ratings." *Journal of Applied Psychology,* 1979, *64,* 502–508.

Jacobson, R. L. "Panel Offers Advice for Trustees and Aspiring Presidents." *Chronicle of Higher Education,* Sept. 26, 1984a, p. 27.

Jacobson, R. L. "Strains of the Job Limit Presidents' Role, Panel Says." *Chronicle of Higher Education,* Sept. 26, 1984b, p. 1.

Jacobson, R. L. "Trustees, Vexed Over Colleges' Quality, Said to Mull Role in Academic Affairs." *Chronicle of Higher Education,* Feb. 20, 1985, p. 1.

Kantor, R. *The Change Masters.* New York: Simon & Schuster, 1984.

Kaplin, W. A. *The Law of Higher Education: A Comprehensive Guide to Legal Implications of Administrative Decision Making.* (2nd ed.) San Francisco: Jossey-Bass, 1985.

Kauffman, J. "Presidential Assessment and Development." In C. F. Fisher (ed.), *Developing and Evaluating Administrative Leadership.* New Directions for Higher Education, no. 22. San Francisco: Jossey-Bass, 1978.

Kauffman, J. *At the Pleasure of the Board.* Washington, D.C.: American Council on Education, 1980.

Kavanagh, M. J. "Evaluating Performance." In K. M. Rowland and G. R. Ferris (eds.), *Personnel Management.* Newton, Mass.: Allyn & Bacon, 1982.

Keller, G. *Academic Strategy—The Management Revolution in American Higher Education.* Baltimore, Md.: Johns Hopkins University Press, 1983.

Kerr, C., and Gade, M. L. *The Many Lives of Academic Presidents: Time, Place, and Character.* Washington, D.C.: Association of Governing Boards of Colleges and Universities, 1986.

Kimble, G. A. *The Department Chairman's Survival Manual.* New York: Wiley, 1979.

King, L. M., Hunter, J. E., and Schmidt, F. L. "Halo in a Multidimensional Forced-Choice Performance Evaluation Scale." *Journal of Applied Psychology,* 1980, *65,* 507–516.

Klumph, N. L. "Management's Seven Deadly Sins." *Piedmont Airlines Magazine,* Feb. 1986, pp. 39–42.

Kondrasuk, J. N. "Studies in MBO Effectiveness." *Academy of Management Review,* 1981, *6,* 419–430.

Kopolow, L. E. "Stress: Recognizing It and Coping With It." *Executive Productivity,* June 1987, 7 (6), 2–3.

Kotter, J. *Power and Influence.* New York: Free Press, 1985.

Kram, K. *Mentoring at Work: Developing Relationships in Orga-nizational Life.* Glenview, Ill.: Scott, Foresman, 1985.

Lahti, R. E. "Managerial Performance and Appraisal." In C. F. Fisher (ed.), *Developing and Evaluating Administrative Lead-ership.* New Directions for Higher Education, no. 22. San Francisco: Jossey-Bass, 1978.

Landy, F. J., Farr, J. L., and Jacobs, R. R. "Utility Concepts in Performance Measurement." *Organizational Behavior and Hu-man Performance,* 1982, *30,* 15–40.

Latham, G. P., Wexley, K. N., and Pursell, E. "Training Man-agers to Minimize Rating Errors in the Observation of Behav-ior." *Journal of Applied Psychology,* 1975, *60,* 550–555.

Lawler, E. E. *Pay and Organization Development.* Reading, Mass.: Addison-Wesley, 1981.

Lee, B. "The Pursuit of Excellence in Lecturing Staff—Mentor-ing and Mutual Development Groups." *ASTD Newsletter* (Loughborough University of Technology, England), Autumn 1986, p. 15.

Leibowitz, Z. B., Farren, C., and Kaye, B. "The 12-Fold Path to CD Enlightenment." *Training and Development Journal,* 1985, *39* (4), 28–32.

Lindquist, J. "Approaches to Administrative Development: A Synthesis." In J. A. Shtogren (ed.), *Administrative Develop-ment in Higher Education.* Richmond, Va.: Higher Education Leadership and Management Society, 1978.

Llgen, D. R., and Barnes-Farrell, J. L. *Performance Planning and Evaluation.* Chicago: Science Research Associates, 1984.

Locher, A. H., and Teel, K. S. "Performance Appraisal—A Sur-vey of Current Practices." *Personnel Journal,* 1977, *56,* 245–247.

Lombardo, M. M. "Questions About Learning from Experience." *Issues and Observations,* 1986, *6* (1), 7–10.

Lucas, A. "Effective Department Chair Training on a Low-Cost Budget." *Journal of Staff, Program, and Organization Devel-opment,* 1986, *4* (2), 33–36.

Lynch, D. M., Bowker, L. H., and McFerron, J. R. "Leadership in the Liberal Arts: A Study of the Concerns and Job Experiences of Chief Liberal Arts Academic Officers." Paper presented at annual meeting of American Educational Research Association, San Francisco, Apr. 1986.

McCall, M. W., Jr. "Design and Implementation of Appraisal Systems." In D. DeVries, M. McCall, and S. Shullman (eds.), *Performance Appraisal Workshop: Briefing Book.* Greensboro, N.C.: Center for Creative Leadership, 1978a.

McCall, M. W., Jr. *Power, Influence, and Authority: The Hazards of Carrying a Sword.* Technical Report, no. 10. Greensboro, N.C.: Center for Creative Leadership, 1978b.

McCall, M. W., and Lombardo, M. M. "What Makes a Top Executive?" *Psychology Today,* 1983, *17* (2), 26–31.

McCurdy, J. "Several Trustees of Cal. State U. Said to Seek Ouster of Chancellor." *Chronicle of Higher Education,* Apr. 8, 1987, p. 15.

McKenna, D. L. "Recycling College Presidents." *Liberal Education,* 1972, *58* (4), 456–463.

McMillen, L. "Breaking the Cycle of Paperwork and Meetings." *Chronicle of Higher Education,* June 18, 1986a, p. 28.

McMillen, L. "Most Effective College Presidents Are 'Risk Takers' Who Rely on Respect, Not Popularity, Study Finds." *Chronicle of Higher Education,* Nov. 5, 1986b, p. 11.

"Management Wisdom." *Academic Leader,* 1986, *2* (6), 2.

Many, P. "Academics Should Learn the Fine Art of Saying No." *Chronicle of Higher Education,* Nov. 19, 1986, pp. 48–49.

Marchese, T. "Learning About Assessment." *AAHE Bulletin,* Sept. 1985, pp. 10–13.

Marist College Review and Planning Evaluation Manual, Jan. 1987, pp. 1–8.

"Mason University: Twenty-Nine, Growing Fast." *New York Times,* Dec. 31, 1986, p. 15.

Mauer, G. J. (ed.). *Crisis in Campus Management: Case Studies in the Administration of Colleges and Universities.* New York: Praeger, 1976.

Meyer, H. H. "The Annual Performance Review Discussion— Making It Constructive." *Personnel Journal,* 1977, *56,* 508–511.

Meyer, H. H. "Self-Appraisal of Job Performance." *Personnel Psychology*, 1980, *33*, 291–295.

Miller, R. I. *The Assessment of College Performance: A Handbook of Techniques and Measures for Institutional Self-Evaluation.* San Francisco: Jossey-Bass, 1979.

Miller, R. I. "Improving Administrator Evaluation." Paper presented at the Workshop on Evaluating Faculty, Administrator, and Institution Performance, University of Maryland, Feb. 1985.

Millett, J. D. "Professional Development of Administrators." In C. F. Fisher (ed.), *Developing and Evaluating Administrative Leadership.* New Directions for Higher Education, no. 22. San Francisco: Jossey-Bass, 1978.

"Minn. Judge Releases Part of Magrath Evaluation." *Chronicle of Higher Education*, July 11, 1984, p. 2.

Mondy, R. W., and Noe, R. M. III. *Personnel: The Management of Human Resources.* (2nd ed.) Newton, Mass.: Allyn & Bacon, 1984.

Morris, V. *Deaning: Middle Management in Academe.* Champaign: University of Illinois Press, 1981.

Munitz, B. "Strengthening Institutional Leadership." In C. F. Fisher (ed.), *Developing and Evaluating Administrative Leadership.* New Directions for Higher Education, no. 22. San Francisco: Jossey-Bass, 1978.

Murphy, P. J. "Preparing Administrators for the Twenty-First Century." *Higher Education*, 1984, *13* (11), 439–449.

Nason, J. W. *Guide to the Periodic Review of the Performance of Chief Executives.* Washington, D.C.: Association of Governing Boards of Universities and Colleges, 1984.

Nichols, D. D., and Stuart, W. H. "In Praise of Fewer Administrators." *Journal of Staff, Program, and Organizational Development*, 1983, *1* (2), 33–38.

Nichols, J., and Sharp, B. "The Professional Origin and Support Needs of Leaders in College and University Planning." Paper presented at annual meeting of the Society for College and University Planning, Chicago, July 1985.

Nordvall, R. C. *Evaluation and Development of Administrators.*

AAHE-ERIC/Higher Education Research Report no. 6. Washington, D.C.: Association for the Study of Higher Education, 1979.

Oberg, W. "Make Performance Appraisal Relevant." *Harvard Business Review,* 1972, *50,* 61–67.

Odom, J. V. *Performance Appraisal: Legal Aspects.* Technical Report, no. 3. Greensboro, N.C.: Center for Creative Leadership, 1977.

"Organizational Effectiveness in Higher Education." *NCHEMS Newsletter,* June 1984, p. 7.

Palmer, S. "Too Many Administrators? A Survey of Colleges Provides Some Grist for Those Who Think So." *Chronicle of Higher Education,* Oct. 5, 1983, p. 21.

Patrick, C., and Caruthers, J. K. "Management Priorities of College Presidents." *Research in Higher Education,* 1980, *12,* 195–214.

Phipps, R. A. "Administrative Evaluation Survey." Salisbury, Md.: Salisbury State College, 1975. (Mimeographed.)

Plante, P. R. "The College Administrator in the Marketplace." *Chronicle of Higher Education,* May 29, 1985, p. 72.

Prather, R. L. "Extending the Life of Performance Appraisal Systems." *Personnel Journal,* 1974, *53,* 739–743.

"Presidential Assessments: A Round-Table Discussion." *AGB Reports,* Jan./Feb. 1983, pp. 36–41.

Raines, H. "A Mentor's Presence." *New York Times Magazine,* June 20, 1986, p. 46.

Rein, R. K. "Braving the Wilds to Survive in the Office." *Money Magazine,* July 1983, pp. 75–80.

Reitz, H. J. *Behavior in Organizations.* (3rd ed.) Homewood, Ill.: Dow Jones–Irwin, 1987.

Rice, B. "Performance Review: The Job Nobody Likes." *Psychology Today,* Sept. 1985, pp. 30–36.

Richardson, R. C. "Staff Development: A Conceptual Framework." *Journal of Higher Education,* 1975, *46,* 303–311.

Roach, J. H. "The Academic Department Chairperson: Functions and Responsibilities." *Educational Record,* 1976, *57,* 13–23.

Robbins, S. P. *Management: Concepts and Practices.* Englewood Cliffs, N.J.: Prentice-Hall, 1984.

Rosovsky, H. "The Ups and Downs of Deaning." *Harvard Magazine,* Jan./Feb. 1987, 34–40.

Rubin, I. "Universities in Stress: Decision Making Under Conditions of Reduced Resources." *Social Services Quarterly,* 1977, *58,* 237–250.

Ryan, J. H. "Continuing Education for College and University Administrators or Improving Management Capacity for the Prisoner of Higher Education." Buffalo, N.Y.: American Association of University Administrators, 1976.

Sagaria, M. A., and Krotseng, M. V. "Deans' Managerial Skills: What They Need and What They Bring to the Job." *Journal of the College and University Personnel Association,* 1986, *37,* 1–7.

Sashkin, M. *Assessing Performance Appraisal.* San Diego, Calif.: University Associates, 1981.

Sathe, V. "Implications of Corporate Culture: A Manager's Guide to Action." *Organizational Dynamics,* Autumn 1983, 5–23.

Schulman, C. H. "Fifteen Years Down, Twenty-Five to Go: A Look at Faculty Careers." *AAHE Bulletin,* 1983, *36* (3), 11–14.

Schuster, F. E. *Human Resource Management.* Reston, Va.: Reston Publishing, 1985.

Scott, R. A. "Do Admissions Counselors Read?" *NACAC Journal,* 1976, *20,* 22–27.

Seldin, P. "Faculty Growth Contracts." In K. Eble (ed.), *Improving Teaching Styles.* New Directions for Teaching and Learning, no. 1. San Francisco: Jossey-Bass, 1980a.

Seldin, P. *Successful Faculty Evaluation Programs.* Crugers, N.Y.: Coventry Press, 1980b.

Seldin, P. "Evaluating Administrative Performance." Paper presented at the Arab Institute for Aerospace Technology, Cairo, Egypt, Jan. 1983.

Seldin, P. *Changing Practices in Faculty Evaluation: A Critical Assessment and Recommendations for Improvement.* San Francisco: Jossey-Bass, 1984.

Seldin, P. "Academic Culture." Paper presented at the National Conference on Professional and Personal Renewal, Atlanta, Apr. 1986.

Seldin, P. "Evaluating Administrative Performance." Workshop presented at the College of Mount Saint Vincent, Riverdale, N.Y., Jan. 1987.

Shaw, K. A. "Presidential Assessment: Good Intentions Gone Wrong." *AGB Reports,* Nov./Dec. 1985, 20–23.

Shtogren, J. T. "Reflections on Chairperson Training in Faculty Development." In J. T. Shtogren (ed.), *Administrative Development in Higher Education.* Richmond, Va.: Higher Education Leadership and Management Society, 1978.

Simmons, A. "Letter to the Editor." *Change,* Sept. 1984, 4–5.

Skipper, C. E. "Four Indicators of Administrative Effectiveness." Paper presented at annual meeting of the American Educational Research Association, New York, Mar. 1982.

Spanegehl, S. D. "The Push to Assess." *Change,* Jan./Feb. 1987, 35–39.

Spool, M. D. "Training Programs for Observers of Behaviors: A Review." *Personnel Psychology,* 1978, *31,* 27–35.

Sprunger, B. E., and Bergquist, W. H. *Handbook for College Administration.* Washington, D.C.: Council for the Advancement of Small Colleges, 1978.

Stauffer, T. M. "Academic Administrative Internships." In C. F. Fisher (ed.), *Developing and Evaluating Administrative Leadership.* New Directions for Higher Education, no. 22. San Francisco: Jossey-Bass, 1978.

Stevens, J. R. "The Development of Academic Administrators: A Passive Exercise." *University Education News,* Council of Ontario Universities, 1982, *2* (4), 5.

Stordahl, B. "Faculty Development: A Survey of the Literature of the 70s." *Research Currents,* Mar. 1981, pp. 7–10.

Strider, R. E. "Checking Out Presidential Assessment." *AGB Reports,* Jan./Feb. 1982, 47–59.

Surwill, B. J., and Heywood, S. "Evaluation of College and University Top Brass: The State of the Art." Washington, D.C.: American Association of State Colleges and Universities, 1976.

Thornton, G. C. "Psychometric Properties of Self-Appraisals of Job Performance." *Personnel Psychology,* 1980, *33,* 263–271.

Toombs, W., and Marlier, J. "Career Changes Among Academics: Dimensions of Decision." Paper presented at annual meeting of the American Educational Research Association, Los Angeles, Apr. 1981.

"Training Managers to Rate Their Employees." *Business Week,* Mar. 17, 1980, 178–183.

Tucker, A. *Chairing the Academic Department.* New York: American Council on Education/Macmillan, 1984.

Tucker, A., and Bryan, R. *The Academic Dean: Dove, Dragon, and Diplomat.* New York: American Council on Education/ Macmillan, 1987.

Tucker, A., and Mautz, R. B. "Presidential Evaluation: An Academic Circus." *Educational Record,* 1979, *60* (3), 253–260.

"Two Women Staff Members Sue U. of Vermont." *Chronicle of Higher Education,* Aug. 5, 1987, p. 2.

Uniform Guidelines on Employee Selection Procedures. 43 *Federal Register* 38290, 1978.

Walker, D. E. *The Effective Administrator: A Practical Approach to Problem Solving, Decision Making, and Campus Leadership.* San Francisco: Jossey-Bass, 1979.

Walther, F., and Taylor, S. "An Active Feedback Program Can Spark Performance." *Personnel Administrator,* 1983, *28* (6), 107–111, 147–149.

"Wayne State U. Overruled in Two Discrimination Cases." *Chronicle of Higher Education,* Aug. 5, 1987, p. 2.

Webb, N. J. "The College Presidency Has Rewards, After All." *Chronicle of Higher Education,* Jan. 29, 1986, p. 80.

Wergin, J. F. "Evaluating Faculty Development Programs." In J. A. Centra (ed.), *Renewing and Evaluating Teaching.* New Directions for Higher Education, no. 17. San Francisco: Jossey-Bass, 1977.

Whitcomb, S. W. "When Funds Won't Stretch: Faculty and Organizational Development Projects for Miniscule Budgets." In M. Svinicki, J. Kurfiss, and J. Stone (eds.), *To Improve the Academy.* Austin, Tex.: Professional and Organizational Developmental Network in Higher Education, 1986.

Winstead, P. C. "MBO and Administrator Education." In C. Farmer (ed.), *Administrator Evaluation: Concepts, Methods, Cases in Higher Education.* Richmond, Va.: Higher Education Leadership and Management Society, 1979.

"Women Said to Be More Careful Than Men in Assessing Employees." *Chronicle of Higher Education,* May 7, 1986, p. 7.

Wood, M. W. "Crosscurrents and Undercurrents in the Trustee-President Relationship." *Educational Record,* 1984, *65* (1), 38–42.

Wooten, B. "Using Appraisals to Set Objectives." *Supervisory Management,* Nov. 1981, pp. 31–35.

Zion, C. "Role Definition: A Focus for Administrative Growth and Evaluation." *Journal of the College and University Personnel Association,* 1977, *28,* 5–12.

Index